CHILDREN
OF THE
REVOLUTION

CHILDREN OF THE REVOLUTION

A Spiritual Journey to Burma and Buddhism

Feroze Dada

Foreword by His Holiness the Dalai Lama

Preface by Duncan Baird

Published by

Filament Publishing Ltd

16, Croydon Road, Beddington

Croydon, Surrey CR0 4PA

www.filamentpublishing.com

+44 (0)20 8688 2598

The right of Feroze Dada to be identified as the author of this work

has been asserted by him in accordance with the Designs and

Copyrights Act 1988

ISBN 978-1-912635-10-8

Edited by Andrew Thorman & Duncan Baird

Photographs by Mumu (Farida) Dada

Designed by Roger Walton Studio

Printed by 4Edge

All profits from the sale of this book are the
property of The Inle Trust Charity

The Inle Trust is a Charity registered in England,
number 1154767.

www.inletrust.org.uk

Every morning we are born again

What we do today is what matters most

Buddha

CONTENTS

'Peace comes from within.

Do not seek it without.'

Buddha

FOREWORD

THE DALAI LAMA

Burma's internal conflict in the past several decades has had a drastic impact on the lives of its people. "Children of the Revolution" is an encouraging account of a Burmese monk's effort to alleviate their plight, especially that of the children.

The author, Feroze Dada, gives a moving account of the monk's work and talks about his own efforts to support a school and a care centre for destitute Burmese children started by the monk in his monastery. I offer my prayers for their success.

September 18, 2014

PREFACE

A Spiritual Journey to Burma and Buddhism

*C*hildren of the Revolution is a book of converging worlds. In it you discover the very human weave of courage, perseverance and vision, woven with a delightful touch of humour and surprise. It also has the beguiling pattern of a journey unfolding. And as it unfolds, you learn. And you are inspired.

Children of the Revolution by Feroze Dada is a story which begins with a chance meeting at a family gathering in Burma (Myanmar) with a freedom fighter from the Pa'O region in the northeast of the country, and which then takes you on to a monastery on the shores of beautiful Inle Lake in Shan State. There, at the Buddhist monastery of Phaya Taung, the head monk Phongyi is passionately caring for and teaching more than 600 orphaned and refugee children of the revolutionary wars. You discover that both the freedom fighter and the Buddhist monk are in their different ways forces of nature, or men of action, and while you learn about their lives, you also find the human goodness that shines in the darkness of war, and you witness the path of the dhamma in the world. You cannot fail to be encouraged by Phongyi's example to *'go beyond one's imagination because there is no limit'.*

But at the same time, another story is unfolding, and that is the journey of self-discovery of Feroze Dada, who moves with his Burmese wife MuMu between his metropolitan western life and Taunggyi in the northeast of Burma, where her family live, and in doing so finds a new reality and purpose.

Feroze is a man of action too, as you will discover. And he has written an inspirational story which is all the more powerful when you consider that his reasons for making the journey are literally a world away from what transpired. There are no accidents, the law of karma tells us, but we're not the sole cause of our experiences either.

Children of the Revolution is both an insight and a teaching and, as every journey is, both a surprise and in many ways surprising. At the heart of the book is the orphanage at Phaya Taung monastery and the story of what it gives and is giving is truly remarkable.

The Burma that we are projected into is one that is gradually discovering some freedom and beginning to reform itself as the fledgling government makes its way tentatively along the path to democracy. But the strife and warfare in the country after 1948, leading to the military coup in 1962 and the subsequent oppression by the military of the minorities, meant that life in the provincial districts was often cruelly hard for the villagers, at the mercy of both the factional warring between rival militias as well as their campaigns against the government forces. Regional conflict was often viciously amplified by ideological differences, including the rise of communism in the east, as well as the ethnic and tribal rivalries and the turf wars to control the cash from the lucrative opium trade. In the Pa'O tribal areas of Shan, Kayin and Kayan in the north and east of Burma we discover the emerging country through the eyes of the freedom fighter who, for reasons of anonymity, Feroze refers to by his Pa'O army rank 'Major', who learned his survival skills early in life smuggling cattle across to Thailand in order to pay for his education. He went on to join the PNO, at one time the largest insurgent force in Burma and now the political and welfare arm of the Pa'O, courageously providing valuable assistance in the movement of fighters, supplies and information between their training camps in Thailand and the conflict zones with the government troops.

At the time the young Major was making his way in the world of the revolutionary fighter, the monk Phongyi was returning to the monastery at Lin Lam near Loikaw in his native Shan province, after completing his formal Theravada Buddhist training in Yangon.

Phongyi had endured a desperately hard childhood in a small village called Pinlaung, but had been accepted into the monastery at Lin Lam to further his schooling, and this experience led him to the passionate conviction that only education could help his people – 'the path to enlightenment is through education'. But by the time he returned to Lin Lam the PNO, fighting against the government forces in the mountains around Taunggyi and Inle Lake, had split into two warring factions – the Red Pa'O and the White Pa'O. East of Inle Lake towards the border with Thailand had become a war zone with government forces trying to suppress the Red Pa'O who had allied themselves with the Burmese Communist Party or BCP. Life in the towns and villages became even more precarious and the refugee problems were soon to be overwhelming.

By 1986 a fragile peace allowed Phongyi to start work on his vision and he managed to establish his primary school at Phaya Taung, and the middle school followed by 1993. This was when the monastery opened its doors to the orphans of the wars, and soon there were more than 450 children living at the monastery and enrolled in the school. Life was very difficult, and in particular the feeding of the children was a huge challenge, but nonetheless Phongyi continued to persevere and by around 2004 permission was granted for the opening of a senior school. The numbers of pupils had risen to around 600 by then, all needing food, care and education. No one is turned away.

Phongyi's and Major's stories bring us together with Feroze at Phaya Taung monastery and it is here by the lake that Feroze becomes more than a story-teller; he himself becomes a moving spirit in the vision to help the children.

Always in the background is the hauntingly beautiful Inle Lake, now becoming increasingly fragile with the onset of development. In some ways the lake can be seen as a metaphor for our constantly changing and impermanent world, and Feroze describes the lives of the peoples of the lake, the fishing communities, and the beginnings of the modern culture on the 'eastern shore'. But in a sense, too, it is the lake that embodies the mysterious transience of the world and its preciousness and sacredness.

The monastery at Phaya Taung where Feroze, MuMu and Major shelter from a severe storm on the lake one evening is a place where lives change. Feroze describes how his very moving relationship with the orphaned children of the revolution grows, first from the welcome and shelter extended to him at the monastery, and then increasingly from experiencing the sense of peace and purpose that Phongyi's inspiring example of leadership and support for his community give.

Feroze's view of the world begins to change, and he starts to do what he can to help the children at the monastery, initially by bringing in computers and teaching skills. He recognises the extraordinary achievement of Phongyi in sheltering the children from the wars and providing education and, as their friendship flourishes, he begins to learn from the Buddhist monk some of the wisdom that comes from a true sense of compassion matched to a deep intellect. He begins to understand the true nature of the Perfections or paramitas by seeing them in practice at the monastery. For the reader, there is the joy of participating in this wisdom teaching as Feroze asks Phongyi to help him understand how Buddhism offers a transformative vision about how to live a meaningful life.

There is an energy at the monastery that gathers up Feroze as he glimpses 'the still centre of the turning world' and he asks Phongyi what he can do to help. Realising that the most important thing he can give is the imagination and drive to enable the monastery to become more self-sufficient and help provide for the children, he begins to think about ways of achieving this in a manner that respects the aims and principles that he has found there.

The result is the plan to build a drinking water bottling plant from the natural springs behind the monastery, and Feroze sets to work on the practicalities of realising this. He raises the funds, negotiates his way through the complexities of the permissions, and puts in place the resources for the design and delivery of Ko Yin mineral water. Ko Yin means novice monk. There are two ambitions – to provide health in the community though fresh purified water, and to generate an income to help feed the children at the monastery. The water plant is now operating successfully, as are the sanitation facilities, a medical clinic, and healthcare training school. Work is well under way on a Teachers' Training facility which will provide education, health and healing for the now 1200 children at Phaya Taung.

Children of the Revolution is both an inspiration and a teaching. It unfolds as a flower does. As you are taken along the twin tracks of a journey through a conflicted region, and a personal journey of reflection, gradually what remains with you is a story about Loving Kindness. Appropriately it starts with a family gathering and ends with the family at the monastery. These are the ripples across the lake, ever-widening patterns of mettā as the children are sheltered, fed, educated, and then go into the world.

Duncan Baird
December 2017

ABOUT THE AUTHOR

Feroze Dada was born in Karachi. He has lived and worked for most of his life in London. He has been a qualified chartered accountant and chartered tax advisor. He was the senior partner of his private client tax practice in Mayfair, London for 25 years. Feroze is also a non-executive director of several private companies.. Outside his professional life, Feroze is passionate about cricket and music. He currently performs in his own band, and is an occasional TV interviewer. This is his first book but hopefully not his last.

His wife MuMu (Farida) Dada, photographer, interpreter and guide, was born in Taunggyi, Burma and then lived in Karachi. She currently runs the family's property business in London.

MuMu and Feroze met in London and were married in Pakistan. They have two grown up children, Sumaya and Nadir, and divide their time between their homes in London and Italy.

ACKNOWLEDGEMENTS

To my wife MuMu Farida for showing me the path to Burma, without which this journey would never have begun.

My sincere thanks to Duncan Baird, Andrew Thorman, Susan Mears & Chris Day, for having the wisdom to make sense of my writing.

To my parents Ahmad & Halima Dada for their spiritual guidance and prayers.

My thanks to so many who have already helped, and those in the future who will continue to help The Inle Trust to fulfil its charitable objectives.

Above all, my admiration for the children at Phaya Taung monastery who through their dignity and humility have been the true inspiration for this book.

WHAT PEOPLE ARE SAYING ABOUT THIS BOOK

'This deeply moving book comprises many tales which all help to tell the wider story of a troubled country. These stories, along with vivid descriptions of the land and its peoples, form the backdrop to one of the most inspiring narratives I have read in a long time: the author's quest to help a monastery school become self-sufficient. His determination and compassion shine from the pages. With so much going on this could be a confusing read, but Feroze has structured the story well. It's a good read and a wonderful story; I hope it will succeed in its fundraising aims.'

Jane Mallin
Reviewer

'It is a true story that combines politics, religion, travel, adventure and self-discovery. One of the most unexpected things about it is that the author is a chartered accountant living in London! This is his first book and it turns out that he is a natural writer. It is beautifully written in a prose that is simple, direct and elegant. The story draws the reader in from the first page and is full of surprises - as well as unforgettable characters, such as Major and the Monk.'

Dr. Brian Klug. Senior Research Fellow in Philosophy
Oxford University

'Set against Burma's long and violent struggle for freedom, the author has captured a powerful and compelling story of heroism and hope. At its heart is a personal and often moving journey which will inspire all who read it.'

Andrew Thorman
Radio & Television Journalist

'Viewed through the eyes of a freedom fighter struggling against feudalism and a Buddhist monk determined to build a future for children orphaned through war and disease, Dada sensitively builds a many-layered picture of a country struggling to come to terms with democracy while at the same time losing its innocence in the face of a surge of capitalism.

But this is not simply a book about Myanmar's journey towards a new freedom, with all of the complexity that freedom brings. It is also a story of the author's own journeys: as a Muslim absorbing Buddhist philosophy and as a London tax accountant who finds new meanings in his life by launching a charity that will bring education and hope to thousands of Burmese children. It is a journey that every reader will urge him to complete.'

Nigel Carrington
Vice-Chancellor of University of the Arts

'This is a current-day story interposed with the history of Burma and how little it has been allowed to progress since independence. The author seems to personify the generosity of spirit which somehow has managed to survive in Burma. The book resonates with humanity but also urgent achievement when opportunities brought by outsiders are patiently developed. This book is a triumph of character defined by action. The personalities at the heart of this book have stories to tell that are worthy of world-wide celebration.'
Professor Alan Richardson
Ri Chair of Science in Enterprise

'Children of the Revolution is an inspiring book written by a genuine, inspiring man. The world would certainly be a happier place if we all strive to make a small corner of it a better place just like Feroze did with 'his' children in Burma…'
Joseph Calleja,
Opera Singer

'Words do not express thoughts very well;

Everything immediately becomes

A little different,

A little distorted,

A little foolish.

And yet it also pleases me and seems right

That what is of value

And wisdom

To one man

Seems nonsense to another.'

Buddha

THE STORY BEGINS

'Three things cannot be long hidden:

the sun, the moon, and the truth.'

Buddha

My story begins with my own journey of discovery. I first went to Burma in 2009 – twenty years after the military rulers decided to change its name to Myanmar and end the country's last vestiges of its colonial past.

I went there to meet my wife's family and in the course of exploring the landscape chanced upon what was then a remote and beautiful lake. It was here I encountered a group of people who were to change my life. In the following years I made several return visits to continue the work I was to begin.

Like most journeys, I found myself setting off for one destination only to arrive at another. I thought I was writing one story only to discover others, and each fresh encounter brought profound changes to me in the way I looked at the world. I was beginning to turn the pages on a new and exciting chapter in my own life. As a Muslim living in the UK with a Burmese wife, I was to find myself embracing another culture and creed.

Burma has a turbulent past and uncertain future: Although

the story I am going to tell is principally about a monastery and the orphaned children it shelters, I will begin by giving you some background. It is generally believed that there are at least one-and-a-half million orphans in Myanmar – formerly Burma. This is a country whose inner beauty has been scarred by the ravages of internal strife and decades of repression, and which as a result has been largely isolated from the world for many years. The orphan children of these wars of reprisal and survival are Burma's future, and they became my compass, leading me towards a new and meaningful sense of purpose.

Burma – I will use the name by which most people still know it – is struggling to come to terms with democracy. Though free elections took place in 2010, after fifty years of military rule deep cultural and religious divisions remain. President Thein Sein, who had been the prime minister in the previous military administration with the rank of general, now promised greater freedom for his people. He won international acclaim by freeing Aung San Suu Kyi – known as 'the Lady' – after fifteen years of house arrest and he opened up the country to the outside world. The international community responded in kind. The US and European Union dropped all non-military sanctions and promised development aid. President Obama visited and invited Thein Sein to the White House. Despite this, Burma remains a fragile and volatile country with continued unrest leading to thousands of internally displaced people, and an exodus of economic migrants and religiously persecuted people attempting to flee its borders and shores.

The Buddhist Burman people make up the majority of the population. Others include the Karen, the Shan and the mainly Muslim Rohingya in the Rakhine State. Military offensives to quell years of separatist insurrections officially ended with ceasefires in 2011 and 2012.

But beneath the apparently placid waters lurk dangerous currents of resentment, suspicion and feudal rivalry. A simmering mistrust between Buddhists and Muslims has sparked renewed violence in the northwest. In the elections of November 2015, Aung San Suu Kyi's National League for Democracy (NLD) won a sweeping 80 percent of the contested seats in both houses of Parliament (25 per cent are reserved for the military), which was well more than the majority needed to ensure the presidency. But much uncertainty remains as to how much the military-backed Union Solidarity and Development Party will respect the new transfer of power. The world watches and holds its breath.

An extraordinary country of contrasts, with a lush landscape of mountains, jungle and rivers, Burma is at a crossroads. The country is rich in natural resources including timber, oil, gas and rice, as well as a source of many precious stones such as rubies and sapphires, but its economy is one of the least developed in the world. Corruption is rife, as is large scale trafficking in heroin.

There are many reasons why there are so many abandoned children in Burma. Conflict yes, but also poverty, disease – particularly malaria and TB – and natural disasters such as the devastating cyclone that struck the country in 2008 claiming at least 140,000 lives.

This is the story of the children I discovered at one remote monastery who have survived against the odds. They are the children of Burma's revolution. This story is about just some of them and some of the remarkable people who have devoted their lives to helping them.

All the profits from this book will be donated to the monastery school and orphanage at Inle, Phaya Taung. www.inletrust.org.uk

CHAPTER 1

BEGINNING

'There are only two mistakes one can make along
the road to the truth; not going all the way and not starting.'

Buddha

I thought I had achieved much, but I was wrong. The whole process
of realising what was missing, and then inadvertently discovering
how to live a truly meaningful life, was in itself a remarkable spiritual
journey.

It might never have happened had I not fallen in love with
a woman from Burma. If she had not introduced me to a tribal
warrior. If he had not taken me to a remote monastery. If I had not
met a remarkable monk. And if he had not shown me the faces of
hundreds of children – many of them orphans.

The world I entered could not have been more different to
my own. I had no map, no compass and no real idea where my
adventure was to take me. My destination was clouded by my own
lack of purpose and fulfilment. I sensed that something was missing
from my world. But I had no idea what.

It is easy to accept a successful career and the security it brings as
the basis for happiness. I had spent my entire working life building a

business so that I could afford to bring up my family in comfort. As the Managing Partner of a Mayfair, London, accountancy practice advising high net worth individuals, I could afford to enjoy a lifestyle far removed from that of most people, and a world away from my childhood and upbringing in Pakistan.

My parents were second cousins who were both born in a remote part of British India where they were members of a relatively well-off family trading in grain. They moved to Karachi in Pakistan in 1948 following the country's partition.

I was the oldest of three brothers. My father was a strict disciplinarian and right from the word go I rebelled. We were all sent to a Catholic school – not because my parents wanted us to become Catholics, but because it offered the best education. Religion never played a big part in our lives. We sometimes prayed at the mosque on Fridays, but that was it. Having said that, my father lived his whole life by a strict code of honesty and decency. In the end it proved his downfall when his business collapsed because he wouldn't cut corners which he felt would compromise his integrity. And while I respected my father, I didn't feel I really knew him. There were no hugs, no bonding. He was very distant. My mother became my best friend.

At 19, on my way to becoming a Bachelor of Commerce, I was in a rock band and captain of my college cricket team. I didn't know it then, but my life was about to change dramatically.

It all began after an unfortunate incident involving a girlfriend. Her mother caught me in the house and reported me to the army. Pakistan is an ultra conservative society, and at that time was under martial law. I was accused of breaking and entering and brought before a senior military figure. I knew I hadn't done anything wrong – well, apart from trying to be with my girlfriend! She had invited me into her home, but of course her parents were horrified. I expected my father to be less than sympathetic – but he was brilliant. He hired a top lawyer and the army officer offered a deal. If I admitted breaking into the house I wouldn't go to jail. But I refused to admit to something I hadn't done. In the end they just let me go with a warning. I imagine the girl's family didn't want their daughter's reputation called into question, and so it was a case of expediency.

My father never talked about it. Not then anyway. Instead he packed me off to London to live with some family friends. I thought it was to play cricket. But my father had other ideas. I didn't know much about England. But I did know about Miami! I had seen movies featuring skyscrapers and sunshine. England, I thought, must be like this. Cricket in the sunshine.

You can imagine my disappointment when I arrived at Heathrow Airport to be greeted by serried ranks of tightly packed houses under leaden skies in Hounslow. Driving into the city through fog and drizzle, my heart sank. This was not how I had dreamed my new life would be. It got worse. My father had arranged an interview at a small firm of accountants. Not a cricket club.

Dutifully, I borrowed a suit and turned up for the interview, without any references, a CV or even proof of my degree. The owner, a kindly Jewish man sitting behind a desk piled high with bits of paper, gave me a job anyway. I think he thought it was the only way to shut me up from talking about sport.

Suddenly, I found myself in a strange country, with no friends, and wearing a borrowed suit. English wasn't a problem because that's what we spoke and listened to in the rock band back in Karachi. What was a problem was being a small fish in a very big pond. To escape the confines of suburban London and a nine-to-five existence, I was going to need money.

My big break came when I teamed up with another articled clerk from work called Roger. He was working as a part time night-club bouncer and introduced me to the club management. But being only nine and a half stone I knew I wasn't going to cut it. Roger promptly told them we came as a pair and, after weighing up the arguments, we were hired.

In those days bouncers had to look sharply dressed and so I had two new suits specially made. And that in itself lead to another part-time job, selling suits on commission. My clients were mostly half-drunk Irishmen who would gather outside a pub while looking for work, and needed to look their best not only for job interviews but also for church or bingo on Sundays.

Soon I was making very good money, and also beginning to enjoy a social life. After finishing my articles and qualifying as a chartered accountant, I moved to another firm of accountants and, more importantly, joined Brondesbury Cricket Club. Founded in 1887 and a member of the Middlesex County Cricket League, the club boasts an impressive roll call of alumni, including the former England captain Mike Gatting as well as Sourav Gangulay, Dermot Reeve, Dilip Doshi and Nick Compton...and now, me. I was to play for them for the next 25 years.

My parents had still not been to London. It was to be 10 years before that happened. Instead I returned to see them every couple of years, but the distant relationship with my father didn't change. My brothers were also pursuing careers which would take them overseas; one went to Canada where he now enjoys a successful career as a psychiatrist, and the other is an international pilot.

Meanwhile at work I had become a tax specialist with a well-known London firm, I had bought my own apartment and was driving a BMW. By 1982, just ten years after arriving in London as a directionless and impecunious teenager, I had set up my own accountancy practice.

A pivotal moment in my life came after meeting Imran Khan,

the former captain of the Pakistan cricket team and now one of the Pakistan's leading politicians, who was playing for Sussex County at the time. He invited me to one of his parties – and it was there that I saw and fell in love with MuMu. I was seeing someone else at the time, but I couldn't take my eyes off this beautiful and demure girl who simply took my breath away. We kept being introduced to each other that evening, and met up a few times soon after, but MuMu had to return to Pakistan. It was another six months before I was to see her again. Within ten days of seeing her in Karachi we were married. It was 1984. MuMu packed her bags and followed me to London. It was a huge leap of faith for her.

MuMu was born in Burma but had lived in Karachi most of her life. The story of her upbringing is fascinating. Her father had fought alongside the British in Burma against the Japanese in World War 2, and then walked more than a thousand miles from Burma to India in retreat with the British army. With no job and few prospects he went to work as an assistant to his uncle who had been appointed Burma's first ambassador to Pakistan. He had already married his childhood sweetheart from Taunggyi in Burma.

MuMu's siblings were both born in Karachi but she arrived in the world on a return trip to Burma. Her mother was one of 15 children and today my wife has no fewer than 54 cousins who all still live in Taunggyi.

Her father stayed on in Karachi where Radio Pakistan was looking for Burmese speakers. As a result he became the first presenter on the Burmese service of Radio Pakistan. Meanwhile, MuMu studied psychology at university then joined the Japanese Embassy as cultural officer. The link with Japan was to form part of an extraordinary circle.

Her father was a truly compassionate man – not only had he unofficially adopted a Burmese child, whose mother had been left destitute after arriving in Karachi to marry a man who turned out to be already married, but he also gave shelter to a homeless Japanese man, who lived with the family for 10 years until he died. MuMu's father could never see evil in anyone. His generosity knew no bounds and his love and affection for mankind was unconditional.

The next major event in our lives was the birth of our daughter Sumaya. This was a momentous occasion for two reasons – the overwhelming joy of becoming parents and, coupled to that, the huge emotional breakthrough of finally becoming close to my father.

My parents had decided to come to London for the first time for the birth. Over dinner one night we discussed what had happened in Karachi that night I was arrested. I told him the unabridged truth and it was if a huge cloud had been lifted from his shoulders. Maybe he thought I had lied at the time, or that my story lacked much substance, but now he was smiling and his demeanour changed. The distance between us and the lack of understanding fell away, and we were at last reconciled as loving father and son.

My father had been forced to retire from his thriving grain business relatively young, before he was 45 years old and after working extremely hard. Looking back, it was a combination of stubbornness and pride, and a refusal to bow to commercial pressures he thought compromised his integrity, which had brought it about. I remember being resentful at the time – at the loss of the status and living standards we had once enjoyed as a family. But now I realise how charitable and principled he had been, and always for the right reasons. I came to understand more clearly then how giving can also have its rewards.

MuMu and I have lived together in London for more than 30 years, raised two children, and settled down to a typical English middle-class lifestyle. Our children – Sumaya and Nadir – were both privately educated and enjoy the trappings of a comfortable family home in the leafy suburbs of north London.

I played cricket. I watched cricket and I followed cricket. I also played in a rock band. I still do. I am a Muslim and I am an Anglophile. I go to the gym, I drive a Mercedes and I holiday in Tuscany. But you could also now say I have become a spiritualist: a seeker of wisdom who has learned about compassion and mindfulness from taking the path of the dhamma in faraway Burma.

On the surface, you might have thought that life couldn't be much better, but looking back now, and understanding more fully what living a good and meaningful life can mean, I know I was just starting out. I don't think I realised it at the time, but while I had been raising my family and building my business, I had paid almost no attention at all to finding any real depth of purpose and developing a strength of spirit. I hadn't been taught how, and if there were moments of puzzlement and even dissatisfaction I tended to ignore them. It would be a while before I was ready to recognise that my attachments came at price. For now, it was just that in the quiet moments, from time to time, my achievements, such as they were, seemed only a part of what true fulfilment could bring. It was to be some years before I realised why and how I needed to change, to become truly alive. One day MuMu suggested a different holiday.

'Let's go to Burma,' she said. 'You haven't been there and it's time you met my relatives!'

Burma – or Myanmar as it is now officially called – is one of the poorest countries in the world with one of the richest bio-diverse environments. For more than fifty years, between 1962 and 2011, it was ruled by a military junta and out of bounds to most visitors. It shares its borders with Bangladesh, India, Laos, China and Thailand – neighbours who have all influenced Burma's culture, language and history. It is a country wracked by internal division. There are eight major races and 135 ethnic groups, many with their own dialects.

They have spent decades fighting each other or the military.

I wasn't sure I wanted to go. But what I was to discover made me question my values, and was to change my life forever. This was the beginning. I started to pack.

CHAPTER 2

SENSING

'When you realise how perfect everything is
you will tilt your head back and laugh at the sky.'

Buddha

We arrived in the former capital Rangoon, now renamed
Yangon, and checked into our hotel. The new administrative
capital Naypyidaw is some 100 miles to the north, but the old city is
much like other Asian hubs – a mecca for bright lights and Japanese
cars jostling with the background of its historical past.

Amongst the cacophony of twenty-first century life sits the
majestically peaceful Shwedagon Pagoda – a golden shrine to
Buddha dating from the fourteenth century. It dominates the city's
skyline, soaring to over 320 feet, and is topped by a golden umbrella
encrusted with 83,000 precious stones. The sixty-four smaller
and four larger stupas used for meditation, and the mandala-like
temple, are very beautiful and lead the visitor naturally towards
the contemplation of the sacred. I found myself transfixed and
fascinated. What did it all mean?

My journey had begun.

We were going to Taunggyi, the rural city in the central highlands
where MuMu was born. Many of the roads in Burma are in a poor

condition, and driving long distance is unpredictable and tiring. Road journeys can take a long time, and so we decided to fly. It's about an hour in the air and I was grateful to discover that while much of the country's infrastructure may date from the British colonial pre-war era, Burma's airline system was first-rate with aircraft operating in competition all over the country. Taunggyi is a university city of some 380,000 people and is the capital of Shan state. It had nothing much to write about – but it was MuMu's home.

Burma is predominately a Buddhist country with more than 90 per cent of the population either Buddhist, or belonging to animist Burmese folk religions. It is also home to significant Muslim and Christian populations of around 4 per cent each.

So here I was, a Muslim married to a Burmese, arriving in my wife's homeland for the very first time. I was naturally a little nervous about how I would be received, both by the family and by the country. With Buddhists and Muslims often at each other's throats, I wondered what impact security issues and the Western war on terror would have on a Muslim visitor to the country.

The plane touched down in Taunggyi where we were met by a handful of MuMu's many cousins. Once we had settled into our hotel, MuMu explained that I would be expected to say a few words by way of introduction and that there would be quite a gathering. She was right.

The entire clan – all fifty-four first cousins, most of whom still live in Taunggyi – had turned up for a barbecue at cousin Ngni Ngni's family home. They brought mountains of delicious food and drink, including a lethal homemade rice-based wine as well as some very pleasant chardonnay from a local vineyard. The younger boys had brought guitars, drums and an accordion. It was a moonlit winter's evening and as the sun began to set it became quite cold.

The wine flowed as the band played a selection of popular

English songs from the Fifties and Sixties. Everyone joined in with the singing and we all held hands and danced around the roaring fire. It was a truly emotional and touching family reunion.

I spent much of my time that evening talking to Ahwin Kaw Kaw, the eldest member of the Maung clan. He was about 80, quite short, with a heavily lined face. He stood stiffly upright and looked very healthy for a man of his age. But that wasn't what struck me – it was the way he looked when he spoke. Not just calmly and softly spoken, but there was also a look of total contentment in his eyes and across his face. I asked him what was his secret.

'I have very little but I need even less,' he said.

'But Ahwin, I meant in the spiritual context.'

He gave me a wry smile.

'I do mean spiritually. I am content just to be alive and I thank God for every day that he gives me.'

I made my thank you speech, and Ahwin was nominated to say a few words in reply. He stood to welcome us.

'The tree can only be as strong as the love and nourishment it gets. MuMu, you have come here all the way from London and have brought your family with you; this is the food our family tree needs to become even stronger.'

As the evening drew to an end, Ahwin took me to one side.

'It would be really nice if you could spend a few minutes with me tomorrow, I have a message for you.'

I was up fairly early the next morning and decided to walk from the hotel to his house, which was only 10 minutes away.

Ahwin was sitting outside on the porch drinking tea. He got up and shook my hand and, gesturing for me to sit in the chair next to him, poured me a cup of strong milky sweet tea.

We chatted for a while and he told me how much he liked MuMu's parents and how close he was to her mother, MayMay. He was also very pleased that I had married MuMu, who was one of his favourite cousins. Then he turned towards me and gently squeezed my hand.

'I just wanted to tell you that if you go to the lake it will change your life completely.'

He didn't expand on his thoughts and reverted to small talk again. But I couldn't leave it there. What had he meant? His expression suggested he did not wish to say anything further, not then anyway, and so I let it go.

I had come to Burma without any expectations. It was just a holiday and a chance to get to know MuMu's extended and extensive family. Although we are all Muslim's my family has never embraced religion beyond tokenism. We have allowed the children to follow their own paths and believe that it's more important to follow a code enshrined in honesty and decency. So what happened during my forthcoming adventure was never pre-planned. It was as much a surprise to me as to my family.

That afternoon we were invited to cousin Ting's house for a private lunch. He was a well-known local architect, and he lived in a very smart residential part of Taunggyi, his house perched on a hilltop overlooking, yet secluded from, the town centre. It was an impressive lunch, with at least twenty different dishes. As was customary, neither Ting nor his wife sat with us. They stood around and served us as we ate, replenishing our plates with virtually every mouthful consumed. After lunch we discussed our tentative plans for the next few days, but Ting abruptly announced that he had planned a surprise excursion. A trip to Inle Lake! And so early the next morning we set off on the three-hour drive which would take us to the lake. I couldn't believe it, coming as it did, so quickly after Ahwin's prediction.

Cousin Ting and his wife Sabai had arranged for us to stay with them as their guests at a hotel owned by a client of Ting's, on a remote part of the shore. The hotel itself, like many of the village houses, was built on stilts sunk right into the lakeside shallows, and this gave the visitor an enchanting sense of being poised between two worlds. Some years ago, Ting had stepped in to complete the building after the original architect had suddenly died. In gratitude Ting always had a place to holiday whenever he wanted. He continued to visit and helped advise on the structural maintenance of the hotel while his wife Sabai, who was a doctor, held free surgeries there for the local families.

Sabai always looked rather sad. Ting explained how they had met at school. I learned that she had had a very tragic upbringing. Her grandfather had been a raja within the Shan State and her father, a politician, fought for a federal Shan state side-by-side with the famous PNO leader Bo Kyaw against the Ne Win military government. Sabai's brother had been killed in the fighting and both her parents were rumoured to have been murdered by the opposition regime. Sabai had cried endlessly in school, where she met Ting. He vowed to marry her and promised that he would never make her cry. He kept both promises.

As there wasn't enough room in Ting's car for the four of us, cousin Ngni Ngni insisted that he and his cousin Stanley would drive us to the lake. Ngni Ngni was instantly likeable, a friendly and happy man who was genuinely loved by everyone. He was unusually tall for a Burmese, well-built, and an accomplished sportsman, having played basketball for his country. He now worked as a coach at the local golf and country club. I asked him what he thought of Ahwin's comments about the lake changing my life.

'Ahwin is truly a remarkable man, a palmist and clairvoyant,' he said. 'But he stopped exercising his special gift because he believes foretelling the future (whether good or bad) interferes with the natural balance of life, and therefore cannot be helpful. So what he said to you about going to the lake was very special.'

We set off towards Inle Lake. The journey meant weaving our way along a metalled two-lane highway between lush green hills covered in shrub and deciduous trees. Burma's dependence on Chinese and Japanese imports was visible everywhere, especially in the number of motorbikes which had invaded southeast Asia like a swarm of angry bees buzzing around constantly. Everyone seemed to own one and they all appear to be on the road at once. They raced dangerously between crude Chinese-built lorries laden with timber and agricultural goods, vegetables and rice. The roadside villages were an evolving mixture of modern concrete structures and traditional wooden homes.

Unlike its immediate neighbours, Burma feels less crowded and much cleaner. Life is noisy and bustling, but somehow in and amongst the everyday chaos, there is a sense of order. At about the same size as Texas and with a population of around 55 million, Burma boasts one of the most bio-diverse ecologies in the world. Fully half the country is covered by forest. According to the World Wildlife Fund it is home to more than 1700 species of birds, amphibians, reptiles and mammals including the elusive red panda, the Burmese tiger and the Asian elephant.

Burma is the world's biggest exporter of teak, and includes among its abundant natural resources zinc, coal, oil and natural gas along with precious stones such as rubies, sapphires and jade. There are over a thousand species of butterfly and an incredible seven thousand plant species, including more than eight hundred types of orchid. Much of this beauty remains hidden in densely forested and inaccessible areas. But this natural paradise is under threat from logging and mining.

MuMu insisted that the very least we could do was to pay for the cost of filling up the van with petrol. We sped through several villages and suddenly Stanley stopped the van and backed up under a tree where a few cars were parked near a large steel container drum. This was the petrol station – Burmese style!

We drove south for about an hour and gradually the landscape began to change. Soon we reached the outskirts of the lake. The houses built here had to cater for people making their livelihoods on both land and water, and the considerable rise and fall of the water level during the monsoon season. Most of them were built on stilts and made of wood and woven bamboo.

Inle Lake is one of the most amazing natural sights I have ever seen. It is about 12 miles long by six miles wide and sits 2,900 feet above sea nestling between mountain ranges roughly midway across Burma. Depending on the season, the depth of the water fluctuates between five and fifteen feet, and the lake is partially covered by dense patches of water lilies and water hyacinth.

As we drove towards the lake, we were stopped by some soldiers camped beside a make-do checkpoint, adjacent to an old wartime bunker. They were collecting entrance fees from tourists. Ngni Ngni refused to pay for MuMu on the grounds that that she was a local and had been born there, and in the end the soldiers gave way. This type of tariff was quite common, and I am sure it was a way for the soldiers to supplement their pay.

When we finally arrived at the shore, we transferred to a boat for the journey to the hotel. When I say boat, I mean a canoe. Thankfully this one was fitted with an outboard motor. The six of us, including two crew, sat one behind the other. It would take a further two hours to get to the hotel. The canoes were powered by small single-cylinder Chinese-made engines which drove the propeller via a long shaft. They made a great deal of noise and threw up huge plumes of water and, being so close to the water, you feel you are travelling at a rate of knots, but in spite of this we made only slow headway.

Usually I would have been getting impatient, but I found there was something about being on the lake, or near to the lake, that was immensely peaceful. I was experiencing an inner calm that I hadn't often felt before. If I let my mind wander, it came back to the here and now in a way that rarely happened in my frantic everyday life at home. I tried to capture the moment.

Inle Lake is home to around seventy thousand people called Inthas. Most of them make their living from fishing – there are nine species of fish found nowhere else – and from farming vegetables on the floating gardens. The abundance of food and easy access to the lake comes with an increasingly heavy price though. This natural source of fresh water is becoming polluted, and the floating gardens and water hyacinths are choking the lake. But, with my innocent eyes, on that special day all I saw was the beauty of the lake and the reflected glow of the warming sun on placid waters. Where could you ever find such a calming and beguiling place to pause and wonder?

We continued along the lake, passing several fishermen in canoes, who managed to row standing up with one leg wrapped around the single oar in some strange contortion of their lower bodies. It looked impossible. Apparently they developed the skill as a means of seeing over the reeds and plant life in order to navigate at the same time as allowing them to keep their hands free to work with the nets.

This part of the lake was alive with activity, being the main mooring for both the tourist boats and also the supply point for the various hotels and villages. Local vendors were out in force selling everything from drinks and fruit to sun hats. There was no shoving and pushing or hard selling, as we're used to in many other countries. All was polite and calm – rather like the waters we were crossing.

As we set off, Ting explained that we were about to witness one of nature's most dramatic aerial displays, and handed us some bird feed. Soon we were greeted by a flock of white gulls which seemed to arrive from nowhere. They swooped and dived over our heads in an amazing aerobatic performance in the hope and expectation of a reward – hence the birdseed. It was well-rehearsed, and spectacular, and there was great skill in the way they cavorted and competed with each other to catch the feed. The birds never seemed threatening or demanding and the display lasted for at least fifteen minutes. Like a symphony, it reached its finale and the birds vanished as quickly as they had arrived.

We were almost half a day from Yangon and nearly two days travelling from London, and without dwelling on it at all I had managed to let go of my day-to-day worries and concerns, my busy schedules and plans. I was experiencing a feeling of renewal. The sacred imagery of Yangon, the energy of the adventure, the tranquility of the lake - all were helping me find an unaccustomed inner peace.

After two hours on the water we approached an encirclement of cottages built on stilts around an inner lagoon. As our boat reached the landing stage in front of the hotel reception, we were greeted by several of the staff lined up in immaculate uniforms, smiling, ringing bells and banging gongs. We felt humbled and genuinely welcome.

We were served a welcoming cup of warm green tea and then shown to our rooms. Our bungalow was one of a dozen or so positioned on a raised walkway on the lake, with views clear across the water towards the western mountains. Our room, though sparsely furnished in natural wood, bamboo and teak, was spotlessly clean and extremely comfortable. We sat on the veranda admiring the view. It was magical. We were a world away from London. Instead of incessant traffic noise and a high-rise skyline, we were surrounded by the gentle sound of water lapping against the jetty and a backdrop of silvery shimmering mountaintops.

Ting organised a special lunch. It was a very hot day, so the cold beer added to the elation I already felt in the beautiful surroundings. Towards evening we went to our bungalows to change. The sun was beginning to drop behind the western mountain range – its rays casting giant streaks of orange across the water. The day was rapidly drawing to a close, as was the activity on the lake. The outboard engines of the fishing boats as they made for shore with their catch gradually faded away, and as dusk fell we were left with the soothing music of the breeze in the reeds along the shoreline, and the ripple of water.

The sunset took my breath away. I was reminded of a line from Burmese Days, George Orwell's literary masterpiece about the waning influence of the British in pre-war Burma. 'Beauty is meaningless until it is shared,' he wrote, and I agreed. But beauty like this could only be shared with its creator.

It was New Year's Eve. The management, staff and some guests put on a dance and music show on a makeshift floating stage moored close by. As I watched the starry lights and flashing arcs of fireworks in the midnight sky, dramatically reflected in the waters of the Lake, I discovered something new about myself, a feeling of joyfulness and curiosity, coupled with a sense that something exciting was about to happen.

The next day I was to meet a man who would play a significant part in changing the course of my life.

CHAPTER 3

MEETING

'The mind is everything

What you think you become.'

Buddha

He was introduced to me as Major, the manager of the hotel. But this role masked an incredible past and one which both fascinated and intrigued me. MuMu was well aware of who and what he was. This was a man who was well known in this part of Burma. But I had no idea about his background or the influence he once had and was soon to have on me.

There was something about Major that made him stand out. He had a distinctive, almost superior look. Bold and confident. He commanded attention and had an air of authority. He was probably in his mid-fifties, of average Burmese build, short and slight by European standards, but he exuded great presence. I began talking to him. He was warm and friendly in his approach to us, talking with MuMu, Sumaya and Nadir, but in his conversation there was a slight air of diffidence, as though he felt uncertain in our presence.

As I got to know him better, I learned that he'd spent years a rebel fighter, fighting the military government. He was lucky to be alive. He'd been shot. He'd seen terrible things. But his life had now taken a different path. I became curious to know more. Looking back now, I know that this was the moment that my life began to change. Physically, my world was expanding towards other horizons, and inside I began to feel the first imaginings of a different purpose.

At this stage it's important to reflect a little more on Burma's history. It was under British colonial rule from 1886, as a province of India, until it was invaded by the Japanese during the Second World War. It is estimated that up to a quarter of a million civilians died in the fighting before the Japanese were defeated. Their reign of terror included the forced construction of the infamous Burma 'Death' Railway by allied prisoners of war. But, however brutal the conditions were for the prisoners of war, it was far worse for the native labourers from the surrounding tribes. More than thirty thousand of them perished.

It was the uncompromising and savage nature of the fighting that convinced the Americans they would have to proceed with the construction of the punishing 1,000 mile Stilwell Road – named after General Joseph Stilwell – linking India with China. The price was appalling. It cost the life of one American for every mile of track. Today the road, which had succumbed to the forces of nature, is being revived. The Chinese are embarking on a reconstruction project which in itself is a new form of invasion – this time for Chinese trade.

Burma was granted independence in 1948. But the country has barely been at peace since. Conflict in the region grew out of the frustration that some groups – especially the Shan – felt over the government's refusal to honour a commitment to give them autonomy when the country gained independence. The armed struggle in this region was to last over 20 years. As a major in the Pa'O tribal army, Major had been in the thick of it all.

We chatted for a while, but I was already fascinated. I decided to

try to find out as much as I could about the hidden war and his part in it. I wanted to know what was it like being a guerrilla fighting the Burmese Army. I wanted to understand how the rebel forces were sustained locally, and how they operated, in this remote region - also what they believed in and were fighting for. I waited for him to change the subject but, far from being coy, he seemed eager to share his story. It was, I felt, a kind of catharsis for him.

So Major began to tell the story of his life. There were none of those hesitations and corrections that most of us make when we speak about complex or painful experiences. It was almost as though he was reading from a book or a script, or as if he had fallen into a trance. He held my attention completely.

His father, a rebel just as his son would one day become, was killed fighting when Major was six years old. In time, when Major was 23, the earliest age he could enlist, he went on to join the same tribal Pa'O insurgency group as his father had fought in.

Suddenly Major stopped talking. After a pause, he lowered his voice and whispered.

'I am sorry. They do not like me talking so frankly about my past.'

Looking up, I saw a waiter nudging ever closer to our table and listening to every word Major said. Government observers are everywhere in Burma; in hotels, restaurants – especially the ones that foreigners frequent. They keep their eyes and ears open and report anything that seems to be unusual. After a while it's easy to spot these 'spies' because they make no attempt at subtlety. All the locals know who they are because they tend to stand around pretending to be busy while not actually doing anything; other than eavesdropping that is.

'You have a fascinating story to tell,' I said. 'Will you let me write about it?'

Major thought for a moment then looked at me with a slight smile.

'I am afraid that the government will not like that at all.'

The next day he disappeared, so I didn't get the chance to pick up on where we'd left his story. I hadn't thought much about it at the time, but we had been questioned in some detail by the authorities about our visit to Inle Lake – far more so than about our proposed trip to the coast which was in a much more troublesome area. I wondered if it had something to do with Major.

Before we headed for the coast, for some sun and sand, there was time to explore the area around Inle. Major had organised a boat trip to cover the local attractions and visit some of the traditional craft workshops. Although it is already becoming very touristy around the southern part of the lake, our boat trip provided us with a great introduction to the area and its wider community, and prepared us for the spectacular sights which await the more persistent and intrepid traveller to the remoter parts of the region.

There were all the usual shops selling clothing, silverware and jewellery, lacquerware and tobacco. The women were adept at making bamboo hats. Silk weaving is another important industry, producing high quality handwoven and distinctive fabrics called 'longyis' – the Burmese name for a sarong.

The lotus plants that grow on the lake produce a unique fibre used to weave the special saffron robes worn by the monks. Needless to say, as commercial interests begin to exploit every possible opportunity, these are now sold to the public. It takes one month and four thousand lotus stems to make just one scarf, which then sells for around $300. That's an enormous sum when the average annual income in Burma is less than $200.

Another abiding image associated with Burma is that of the Padaung women who appear to elongate their necks by wearing a succession of gold or copper rings. The Padaung traditionally live along the Thai border. Sadly these beautifully adorned women are now more often employed as tourist attractions. Legend has it that when the Padaung moved from China to settle in the jungle regions of North East Burma there were many tigers and wild animals roaming about and, in order to protect their women, the tribesmen wrapped them with golden helical rings.

These days gold has been replaced by brass and the rings restricted to their necks and legs. They are considered symbols of great beauty. Usually the first rings are placed at the age of five and are consistently added to until they number the maximum of sixteen rings, by which time the neck has reached its maximum elongation of some twenty-five centimetres. There is an argument that says their necks don't actually stretch – rather their shoulders are pushed down giving the illusion of elongation. Either way, seeing them in their natural village surroundings is a very memorable experience.

We also stopped by the Burmese cat sanctuary. Paradoxically, Burmese cats are now virtually extinct. Imagine our dismay when we discovered that the sanctuary has been importing pedigree stock from the UK and Australia in order to try and re-establish the breed in Burma.

After our sightseeing diversion on the lake, it was time for us to go to Ngapali beach to relax before the long return journey to London. The flight from Heho to Thandwe airport in Rakhine State took about an hour. The beach is about four miles from the town and is the country's most famous resort. I can see why.

It is also not far from an area where some of the most violent clashes between Muslims and Buddhists have taken place. Sadly this enclave of seaside sophistication is adjacent to some of the poorest and most volatile areas of the country bordering Bangladesh. There has been a recent history of violence born of cultural enmity and deprived economic and social conditions. Because of this, Ngapali is not as well publicised as other beaches in South East Asia but, in my view, it ranks among the very best. Its beautiful sandy beach stretches for three kilometres along the Indian Ocean in the Bay of Bengal, and along this shoreline there are some truly luxurious hotels.

Ngapali is not a Burmese name and it is believed to have originated from early Italian travellers arriving there, and comparing it to the beauty of the Bay of Naples. It was once a thriving pearl fishing centre but today its pristine waters are home to squid fishermen and a growing catch of foreign visitors. It can only be a matter of time before the cruise ship industry discovers this paradise, and then much of the charm will be lost forever.

After relaxing at Ngapali we flew to Bagan, an ancient city not far from Mandalay. It covers some 16 square miles on the eastern bank of the mighty Irrawaddy River – now renamed the Ayeyarwady. Bagan was founded in the ninth century. It became the regional capital, home to more than 10,000 temples, pagodas and stupas.

King Anawrahta ruled here between 1044 and 1077, and introduced Theravada Buddhism, or the Teachings of the Elders, which quickly became predominant throughout South-East Asia.

Unfortunately Bagan also sits on a major fault line and as a result it has suffered a great deal from earthquake destruction over the centuries. The most recent earthquake was in 1975 which seriously damaged many of the historical sites. Many people, whose flimsy homes were swept away, ran for shelter and then chose to live in the temples, often destroying centuries of priceless frescos and other historical relics. In 1990 the government forced them out of the old city to a new residential area. Today around 2,000 monuments remain, many undergoing restoration – although, sadly, the repair work undertaken is not always an improvement. For me, Bagan is the eighth wonder of the world. To watch the sunset over the distant mountains casting its rays across the river, and the soft evening light illuminating the plain, littered with these temples, is one of the most hauntingly beautiful sights imaginable.

As we sat on the steps of the Shwesandaw Temple, I kept thinking about what I was experiencing here. I watched the fading of the day and the lengthening shadows on the ancient sacred buildings. Almost for the first time in my life, I felt open to the sensation of something sacred and deeply peaceful. It had little to do with the fact that I was on holiday. There was a serenity about this country – yes, there was violence here too, both past and present – but something gentle and timeless had entered my world. It had become a part of me now, as witnessed by the wordless minutes and hours I spent in that place.

I was on a spiritual journey – I just didn't know it then.

CHAPTER 4

LISTENING

'We are what we think.

All that we are arises with our thoughts.

With our thoughts, we make the world.'

Buddha

On my return to London, I couldn't stop thinking about our wonderful trip to Burma and my promise to Major to write the book about his life. Recalling the feelings of peacefulness I had experienced on magical Inle Lake and at Bagan, I began to read more about Theravada Buddhism, the culture and history of Burma, and to talk with friends about my new feelings and different directions. I was feeling a change of pace and sensing that while my busy working life and my time with my family continued to be absorbing, there was unfinished business in Burma, both in terms of inner and outer happiness. I couldn't describe it at the time, but I felt a gradual awakening to a new purpose.

I thought hard about what had happened, and talked about Burma to MuMu. I knew I would return, and not solely because of her family. There was something else pulling at me. I was completely incapable of articulating it clearly, and so I decided to continue with my practical theme and try to see Major again and do some more interviews. Some months later I emailed him and suggested we meet up in Yangon. I had a pretty good idea that his emails were censored, and communications between us were slow – it was some time before I heard back. Eventually he replied to say that he had arranged to escort a renowned Singaporean monk and his entourage on a visit to a monastery at Inle Lake. That was where we would meet.

MuMu and I arrived in Yangon on December 14, 2011. We felt that much had already changed since our previous visit. In a way the most noticeable change was constitutional. The name of the country had officially become Myanmar in 2008, and in 2010 a new national flag was adopted. This featured three horizontal bands of colour – yellow, green and red, adorned by a five pointed star. Each colour represents one of the themes underpinning the country's new ethos: solidarity, peace and tranquility and courage and decisiveness. The white star stands for the significance of the union of the country.

There was also an undeniable atmosphere of optimism. The pro-democracy leader Aung San Suu Kyi was preparing to take part in the forthcoming election for some 45 parliamentary seats, and the military government had made a conciliatory move by ordering the release of a thousand political prisoners. President Thein Sein had already held a promising meeting with Hillary Clinton and the Burmese media reported news of a similar meeting with the European Union.

With its hard-working, literate and ethical workforce, Burma was preparing to open its doors for business. Of course, China had already kicked open the back door. This was evident from the many construction hoardings, car showrooms and part Chinese-funded major government infrastructure projects to be seen everywhere.

The next day we flew to Heho and took a boat across the lake to the hotel, making sure to stock up on bird feed en route. The lake was so beautiful that I felt blessed to be making this trip once again. On arrival we were greeted by what I can only describe as a kitchen band with staff seemingly picking up anything that came to hand – even pots and pans – to ring out their welcome. After a brief rest we made our way to reception to let Major know we had arrived. I ordered some beers, and we chatted for a while before agreeing to meet the next morning.

The lake was quite cold during the night and early morning, but soon the sun was edging upwards, burning off the morning mist. With the crystal skies emerging, it began to get warm. I felt good about the day, and starting work again on my new project, and so we settled down and Major told me his story. Little did I know then, but his story was to become my story in the most extraordinary way.

Major was one of eight children, of whom only four survived. They came from the same town as MuMu – Taunggyi. His parents were poor farmers and Major, as the eldest, was left to look after his siblings while his parents worked the land. During WW2 his father joined the British Army as a military policeman. After the Japanese surrendered, his father joined the local tribal army, the Pa'O, which was fighting for freedom from serfdom and a system of feudal rule.

In 1958 the Pa'O organisation agreed a truce with the government which, by that time, had done a deal with the feudal Sawbwas, the local chiefs or hereditary princes. When the peace process started, the government began providing schooling and medical facilities in the villages. There was some progress for the Pa'O people but it was short lived.

On March 2 1962, the military led by General Ne Win took control of Burma through a coup d'état and the oppression of the minorities by military means was re-established. On the one hand the government did make some practical changes in order to win over the local people, but on the other hand it was busy eliminating opposition leaders. It did so by inviting the Pa'O leaders to come forward so the two sides could have talks, but once these individuals were identified they either never returned from the talks or subsequently disappeared.

And so the second Pa'O uprising began. Major's father joined up again and fled to the jungle from where the Pa'O organised guerrilla attacks against the Tatmadaw, or Burmese government forces.

It was during one such encounter that his father was killed. He was one of the first to die in a government attack on their jungle base, leaving his wife with eight children, including two sets of twins. Major was just six years old at that time.

No one in his unit was prepared to break the news to his family and it was almost a year before his mother was told. Both sets of twins later died from malaria. There were no medical facilities. Major's mother is still alive at the age of seventy-three. She married three more times. Major was taken in by his uncle who sent him to the village primary school at Nampan on Inle Lake.

Major's school days were cut short by the second Pa'O insurrection, which started with vicious fighting in the Pa'O villages in the mountains to the east of Inle, and north near Taunggyi. As part of the reprisals, the government withdrew all funding for education programmes, meaning there was no money for teachers' pay or for upkeep of the school, which rapidly fell into serious disrepair. Eventually only the headmaster remained. With hardly any food, the boys became desperate. A cow wandered into the crumbling school and provided a most welcome meal – but when the headmaster was forced to pay compensation that exhausted the last of the funds and the school closed. Once again the children were abandoned.

When he was fourteen, Major was handed over to the nearby

primary school at Patama Mine Pyo monastery in the Nyaung Shwe township at Mine Pyo village in Inle, where he became a student and helper to one of the monks.

One day there was a commotion in the village. Apparently the local BCP (Burma Communist Party) had been raided by the military police. They were attempting to recapture a BCP activist who had managed to escape after being wounded in crossfire.

Later that night Major heard whimpering, like a wild animal in pain. He went out with the intention of rescuing it but when he opened the door of an outhouse he found a man covered in blood and lying unconscious on the floor. Major dressed his wound with strips of bandage made from his shirt and then alerted the monks.

It transpired that the man, whose name was Ti Hha, had been shot in the shoulder and had lost a lot of blood. Thanks to Major's rapid intervention he was at least still alive, but he would need urgent medical attention. Major pleaded with the monks to give him sanctuary and promised he would personally tend to him. The monks reluctantly agreed to take the man in even though they realised he was a terrorist. As a wanted man there was no possibility of Ti Hha getting any medical help from the hospital. And so Ti Hha stayed at the monastery with Major taking on the role of chief nurse. Without specialist hospital treatment it was touch and go, but after several weeks the man recovered.

On sitting up in bed, the first thing he asked Major to do was to fetch some rice wine. Fortunately Ti Hha had some money and so that evening Major managed to buy enough wine to not only intoxicate Ti Hha but also half a dozen of the monks' other young helpers. The quiet tranquility of the monastery was briefly transformed as they drank and laughed the night away.

This was the young Major's introduction to both alcohol and a hangover. It was a rite of passage for a while as he accompanied Ti

Hha on his drinking and womanising sessions. But Major found he didn't have the stamina to burn the candle at both ends. He kept falling asleep in lessons and neglecting his duties at the monastery.

Inevitably it wasn't long before Ti Hha was exposed and banished from the monastery forever. But along the way, Major had grown into a man, aware of the dangers of the political world outside the monastery, and the need to find his own future.

Major left the monastery when he was sixteen. He went back to live with his uncle in Taunggyi and continue his education there. But money was tight and he needed to find a way to make ends meet. I couldn't help but remember my own experience after arriving broke in London and needing to find a way to fill my pockets. My parents were thousands of miles away and I was living on my wits. Major was going to have to do the same. And in doing so his life was about to change again.

He had six months before starting college and he knew he had to make some serious money if he was going to survive. His opportunity came when he overheard a man in the local market who was buying cattle to take to Thailand. He was curious. It transpired that not only did the man want to buy cattle, but he was looking for strong young men to help him take them across the hills and through the jungles and rivers, before smuggling them across the border at Mae Hong Son into Thailand. Major struck a deal and in the next few weeks helped him recruit a group of thirty or so men and buy a hundred-and-fifty head of cattle from various markets in and around Heho and Taunggyi. So he became an outlaw, a wanted man, living dangerously and working the smuggling route between Burma and Thailand.

It was a perilous but potentially lucrative venture. Success would bring relative riches – but failure would have devastating consequences. A round trip would take them between two and five weeks depending on the weather and level of security. They lived on raw rice, dry spices, salt and chillies which they carried wrapped in a cloth slung over their shoulders like a bag. Cooking was done using ex US ration tins. They each took a piece of plastic sheeting which served as a ground-sheet, table cloth and raincoat, along with a rope, a knife and matches.

They would walk throughout the first night until reaching the first major obstacle, the Phon River. The bridges were all patrolled by soldiers so they had to find a remote place to swim across. The river was about waist deep and 15 metres wide. Although the cattle could swim, most of the men couldn't, and so they fixed ropes between each bank to use as guidelines.

During the dry seasons the men had to compete with the cows for drinking water, often relying on stagnant pools left over from the rains. That brought another risk – malaria – since these were breeding grounds for mosquitos. The choice was pretty simple. Risk death from malaria or thirst.

'When you are dehydrated and suffering from intense heat and thirst, the choice becomes a lot easier,' is how Major put it.

It wasn't just the government troops they had to avoid. The minority tribal forces hassled them for money along the way in return for safe passage. I heard how the BCP (Burmese Communist Party), the WNA (Wa National Army) and KNPP (Karenni National Progressive Party) were all operating in the area, either fleeing from persecution or fighting government forces, or indeed each other. They competed to collect taxes or smuggle opium to fund their insurgent activities. Apparently the going rate for safe passage was around 5000 kyats ($5) per cow. The WNA was very organised and controlled the main river, the Salween, that needed to be crossed. For a price the men were allowed to use their canoes.

This was the most dangerous crossing, especially in the rainy season when the water was extremely deep and often very rough. It was not possible to cross by wading or swimming. Using boats hired from the WNA, each man sat with a cow submerged in the water alongside. The animals were tethered to the boats using ropes passed through their pierced nostrils. And to stop them panicking and being swept away by the fierce current, the men would comfort them by holding onto their heads.

It must have been an extremely frightening experience both for the men and the cows, and wasn't without its tragic moments. It could take several days to get all the animals across and on more than one occasion one of the men was swept overboard never to be seen again.

Avoiding the government forces was uppermost in their minds – to be caught would mean instant execution. The troops were on constant lookout for insurgents and often engaged in fierce gun battles with them. An advance party was always sent several miles ahead to warn of any danger. On one occasion the army followed the cattle footprints and were easily able to catch up with them and their slow moving herd. The men had to abandon the livestock and run and hide in the jungle.

It was during one such adventure that Major and his unit were ambushed and he was shot and wounded in the stomach. He was taken to hospital in Taunggyi where the doctors were told he was suffering from a stomach ulcer. The nurse who treated him was a young trainee called Thaé Mar, and during the time of his convalescence they fell in love. They married once Major had finished his university degree and Thaé Mar had completed her training as a nurse. Major was truly smitten, and remains so to this day.

After recovering from his wounds, he was to make several more trips across the border, all the time risking his life. Listening to him describe his dangerous path, I recognized it was literally a world away from my financial struggles in London, but deep inside I felt a kinship with Major and wanted to learn more about him. As young men we had shared a common goal – to earn money in order to make something of our lives. But now I wanted to understand something deeper about his resourcefulness, and his way of living. I instinctively felt that somehow Major would guide my footsteps along new ways, as indeed he did. Our paths had crossed and then, without realising it at first, we began to share a common goal.

Smuggling was, and still is, a way of life for impoverished Burmese villagers. They would sell or barter what they had – fruit and vegetables – in return for other basic essentials such as cooking oil and cooking utensils. Today the same trade persists but the goods are quite different. Gemstones, drugs and teak are routinely smuggled, especially into China. Elsewhere it's human trafficking and often with terrifying consequences. As Burma's economy emerges from decades of military rule, and US and European sanctions are eased, so the situation will hopefully improve. But despite the outwardly obvious signs of international investment and new construction projects, especially in Yangon, much of the country is still very far behind the progress of its neighbours in India, Thailand and China.

The economy remains one of the least developed in the world, suffering from the effects of decades of stagnation, mismanagement and isolation. Among the major economies, to date only China, India and South Korea have invested substantially in Burma.

The rich architectural and spiritual heritage of its Buddhist culture has hugely boosted Burma's increasingly important tourism industry. This is perceived to be one of the key areas for any future foreign participation and investment. But religious tension between Buddhists and Muslims continues. Constant flare-ups in fighting, as well as political uncertainty, deter many potential visitors.

It was time to explore. Major had arranged for a four-wheel drive to take us from Inle Lake across the mountains to the surrounding Pa'O villages and onwards towards Taunggyi where MuMu planned to meet up with her cousins. Virtually the whole fifty miles or so of the journey was on dirt roads that would have been impossible in an ordinary car. The driver, who had been a truck driver for the Pa'O, was in his element in this terrain, negotiating the deeply rutted and muddy tracks that linked the villages. Although there is a well-defined infrastructure of roads in the country, many are in a very poor state of repair. You can be driving along a surfaced road one minute, and the next find yourself negotiating a cart track. You are as likely to encounter an ox and cart as a Land Cruiser. There were several detours to, as Major put it, avoid any awkward situations, by which he meant encounters with military patrols. The landscape was lush with forests and, in between, crops seemed to have been planted everywhere.

We could see people bathing and washing clothes in the many streams. The Pa'O are distinctive because they mostly dress in black. This is based on their belief that they are descended from Nagah, the mythical dragon. They also wear their clothes layered like the scales of a dragon. In contrast they wear colourful headgear. We could see many examples of this on the men and women who were working side by side in the fields wearing red, orange, blue and green headscarves. It always amazes me that in a country where families exist on less than a dollar a day, the children are neatly dressed in smart school uniforms and their parents wear such elegantly simple and graceful clothes.

Major stopped at a few huts along the way to visit families and check on the progress of the welfare work he had been carrying out in the area – helping to find work for young people at the hotel or in the towns, and organising funds to provide for their education. He was clearly still deeply involved in fighting their corner, though now in a peaceful way. He was obviously well-known and hugely respected.

We finally reached Major's village and stopped at a house, where we were invited to sit around the fireplace, and served green tea blended with roasted sesame seeds, its welcoming aromatic flavour reflecting the family's warm smiles. The grandmother shook hands and was amazed how soft my hands were. She beckoned the rest of the family to come over and have a look – each one had to have a feel and discuss them animatedly before I was given a nod of approval and allowed to sit down. My years of office work had placed me a long way from their lives in the fields. Without knowing how, I hoped I could make my hands useful for them.

There were no modern amenities in the village, no electricity, TV or landline telephones. We were expected to remove our shoes before entering the one large communal room, which served as a living room and kitchen by day and a bedroom by night with the family sleeping on the rush floors. Interestingly there were no animals of any sort in the village, either pets or livestock. Instead they bought their meat from local markets. This may have had something to do with their attitude to cleanliness.

Major explained how the government had built a new hospital in the area but that it was often practically empty. To ensure it wasn't closed down due to the lack of patients, the villagers dutifully turned up pretending to be ill before any government inspection.

The Pa'O are a handsome and dignified people who possess a sense of serenity etched on their kind and open faces – expressions that we in a world of plenty sometimes seem to have lost.

There was always so much to explore, both in terms of the

way of life and the country itself. Having now visited some of the mountainous areas, we wanted to venture further into uncharted waters, travelling to the furthest shore of the lake. This involved a three-hour boat journey of over 25 miles heading south through the long channel from Nampan towards Samkar.

After an hour we stopped to visit the market at Mawbe. As we approached we were greeted by a flotilla of small boats filled with pretty smiling girls offering us jewellery and ornaments, all eager to try and catch us before we landed. There was no hard selling by our reception party. The girls were happy and laughing and, if we chose to buy, they were over the moon – if not, they still smiled. In many ways their presence felt more like a welcoming committee than a sales presentation.

Markets were a key part of the local trading tradition and boats of all shapes and sizes jostled for space around the crowded landing areas. Our boatman tried to get us as close as possible, but in the end the only way to reach the shore was by hopping from boat to boat.

This was where members of the Intha tribe brought their fish and vegetables to barter or sell in exchange for grain and meat from the Pa'O people. A few stalls sold trinkets for tourists, but this was mainly a market for locals. We stayed a short while, took some pictures and drank some green tea, then set off again on our journey south.

After a few minutes we reached Mawbe Bridge. We were stopped by some uniformed troops stationed on the bridge overhead. One of them lowered a basket to us on a rope and Major put some money into it. A few words were exchanged with the senior officer via the walkie-talkie that Major was carrying. There was obviously some sort of established understanding between Major and the soldiers, and so without further delay we were allowed to continue.

After another hour or so we stopped again – this time at Samkar (also called Sankar and Samka) with its enchanting and haunting ruined stupas – many of which had trees and jungle foliage growing through them. This village had been off-limits for many years but it is now possible to visit with a guide. At one stage it must have been an impressive site featuring dozens of once-ornate stupas. Today it is still arresting – but for a different reason. Its stupas have largely fallen into disrepair and remain only as a crumbling reminder of past glories. The only other living creature among these ruins was a grazing cow.

Quite nearby there was an altogether different attraction: an illicit brewery that distilled rice to produce various lethal alcoholic drinks. It would have been impolite to refuse to sample a drop or two before heading for home, stopping for a sumptuous local feast on the way and arriving late in the evening at the hotel in Nampan, exhausted but exhilarated. I was becoming intoxicated with this country and its people. There was much to discover and learn, and I was already listening.

The next day Major had to leave unexpectedly, apparently for an emergency meeting with the Pa'O. Our journey of discovery was once again put on hold, but I felt sure it wouldn't be long before we would meet again.

CHAPTER 5

DISCOVERING

'Your work is

to discover your work

and then with all your heart

to give yourself to it.'

Buddha

As we prepared for our third trip to Burma, the world's front
pages were plastered with the pictures of President Obama
embracing Aung San Suu Kyi. The US President spoke of rewarding
the regime by opening up trade links, and stressed the importance
of embracing the various minority communities within Burma – a
reference to the violence between Buddhists and Muslims in the
State of Rakhine.

Corruption remained rife, and the decision to open the country's
borders to mass tourism and benefit from foreign currency inflows
had led to some unscrupulous and unregulated profiteering. There
were stories of how civil servants were demanding significant
donations to monasteries before approving business licenses. Many
of these transactions were apparently negotiated over a round of
golf. So much seemed to be changing. We wondered how much of
its traditional character the country would lose as it emerged into
the light of the modern world.

We had returned to London at the end of the year, promising

ourselves another visit to Inle Lake before the following summer. This was to be a short trip to meet more of MuMu's family, and to spend time with Major and finish writing his story. We arrived in the evening of the second day after flying in to Yangon and catching one of the interconnecting flights north.

The lake looked beautiful in the dying moments of the setting sun. But MuMu's cousin Ting explained that it was beginning to shrink because of encroaching vegetation spreading across the surface as a result of the intensive use of fertilizers, and the increasing dependence on the lake for irrigation. It was time to explore more of this magical but fast changing world. Somewhere here was the key that would unlock a whole new beginning for me. I could appreciate the majesty of my surroundings, I could be enthralled and intrigued by Major's stories, and I could be seduced by the gentle charm of the people. But I wanted to discover more.

Could we go even further south, I wondered, beyond Samkar and the clandestine brewery, to the uncharted waters of Inle Lake, which few visitors had been permitted to navigate? Something was drawing me in deeper. At that time tourists were not allowed free access to the whole of the lake. It seemed much of the area was under the quasi-control of local militia and recently there had been a spate of foreigners being robbed. Apparently some Japanese tourists had been kidnapped and held for ransom. Major started to make some arrangements, and after a few hours we were told we could leave for Lwe Paw early the next morning. We were never to get there. Instead we were to reach a turning point in my life.

Lwe Paw was between four and five hours south by boat, depending on conditions. The route meant crossing the main lake then going through the long narrow channel under Mawbe Bridge before entering the wider part of lake again near Samkar. Then it was south through another channel to our planned destination. We set out very early the next morning after some strong coffee. The local coffee produced around Inle Lake is delicious and aromatic, and is far better than most of the upscale blends in the West.

It was a wintery morning. Temperatures could drop close to zero at night but during the day the sun would burn you without the protection of sun cream or an umbrella. Between these extremes the morning mist lay over the lake like a soft white feather duvet. It might take up to two hours for the sun to burn off the mist and for the lake to emerge in all its brilliance.

We had arranged for blankets, windbreakers, and umbrellas, which proved invaluable on the choppy waters of the big lake near Samkar. Our umbrellas protected us from the monsoon rain, the sun during the midday heat, and – if held out horizontally – kept us dry from the spray. We all wore life-jackets on this trip as visibility was poor when we set out and the surface was particularly rough near Samkar.

To begin with it seemed as if the boat was gliding on a bed of clouds. There was no sense of the water – just a distant horizon above the low-lying mist. Instructions concerning the right course through the maze of reeds and water hyacinths were constantly shouted from the lookout at the front of the boat to the helmsman at the stern. Not only had he to steer the right course but also to control the angle of the propeller depending on the depth of water, which was only a few feet in places.

The lake began to come alive at sunrise. On our way we passed lots of small boats, each with two or three children rowing to school, their neat school uniforms of white shirts with dark shorts or sarongs accentuated in the bright morning sun.

We could also see the fishermen laying out their nets and the general hustle and bustle on the lake accompanied by the mellow chanting from the local monastery. The scene was picture perfect with its own soundtrack.

After about an hour navigating through rampant weed and other obstacles we reached Mawbe Bridge. There were some basic facilities there so we were able to take a break. The bridge was patrolled by militiamen stationed at either end. Major walked towards the sentries who clearly recognised him and appeared to greet him like an old friend, though we were too far away to hear what was being said. He returned accompanied by a man who seemed to be in some way associated with the militia.

He quietly took up position in the stern of the boat, which we assumed was to ensure our continued safety and help negotiate our way past other militia posts. Apparently these were the very same soldiers who fought side by side with Major as Pa'O guerrillas during the insurgency, and some of them had even served in his command. Now they formed part of the quasi-government local security force for that area.

We reached Samkar after three or four hours and stopped at a house with a huge veranda that stood on stilts near the middle of the lake. This was the final staging post and watering hole for the most adventurous tourists, and it was as far as we would normally have been allowed to go.

We ordered green tea and some tofu kyaw (fried crispy tofu) snacks to eat, but the main purpose was to choose the menu for lunch on our return. This informal planning ahead allowed the two women who owned the restaurant time to paddle into town to buy fresh ingredients – rice, vegetables and chicken – which would be served with the local rice wine as an optional extra. At over 40 per cent proof it is more like a spirit than a table wine. After a quick break we set off again. In no time the lake widened out and the water became crystal clear. It felt more like being on a river because of the fast flowing current with the little canoe fighting against the waves and the water spraying all over us.

It was time for the umbrellas to come to our rescue. We forged ahead slowly, and in the excitement of it all hadn't noticed that the sun had gone behind some ugly black clouds. The sky became overcast and soon it started to drizzle. We couldn't decide whether to hold the umbrellas vertically or horizontally. Soon the rain turned into a heavy downpour, with rolling thunder and flashes of lightning. The sky became frighteningly dark and visibility was down to a few feet. The boat starting rocking ferociously.

The crew seemed unperturbed and had every intention of pressing on all the way to Pekhon, the furthest point south, a distance of about 50 miles, which is long way in a motorised canoe even in good weather. Being a fair-weather tourist from London with a big interest in self-preservation, I urged them to head for the nearest land. After a bit of persuasion we turned towards the shore.

We were very relieved to reach dry land. By then it was almost pitch black and all we could see through the intermittent flashes of lightning was a large dark old building looming in front of us. As we approached we saw that it was full of children peering curiously out of the windows, with others standing on the veranda, watching to see who these strangers were.

We headed for the door but Major beckoned us to keep going for a few minutes, despite the lashing rain, until we reached another smaller building. Standing at the entrance dressed in old saffron robes was an unusually tall, well-built and handsome monk; he was probably in his early fifties. The monk urged us to enter. He welcomed Major, who he obviously knew, and invited us to come in and sit down. We sat on the floor facing the monk. In no time some novice monks produced hot green tea and some tofu kyaw. After being soaked through by the storm this was very warming and, I have to say, most welcome.

The monk was eager to find out all about us. When MuMu spoke to him in Burmese he seemed impressed, but also curious because he had assumed she was a foreigner. In particular he wanted to know about MuMu's family in Taunggyi. We chatted for an hour or so and he told us that this village had been directly in the middle of operations involving both the Pa'O and the BCP (communists) during the insurgencies and, as a result, had been constantly harassed by the military. The government had cut off all aid to the area and even now they lacked basic amenities.

I was still wondering about the children in that dark building. Who were they and where had they come from? The monk understood my question in English but chose to reply in Burmese.

As he talked with MuMu, I watched our host closely. There was something unusual about him, an aura, a force of energy, a sense of quiet assurance. I was in the presence of an exceptional human being. I felt I had never met anyone like this before – and so it turned out to be. What he told me was to change the course of my life.

He explained how this was a monastery caring for more than 450 children, many of them orphaned by the wars, providing them with shelter, food and education. These were children of the revolution. We went from one building to another, perhaps five in all, in different stages of disrepair but all spotlessly clean. The children attending various classes occupied every room in every building. They were all used for schooling, including the old timber-built monastery.

At night the classrooms become dormitories. We could see that their sole possessions were in boxes neatly stacked up at the side of the room. All of them exactly the same shape, size and colour. The children we met looked content and were well behaved. Everywhere we were greeted by their smiles. No one pestered us or grabbed us or fired questions at us. Instead we were simply objects of mild curiosity. The children kept to their routine – whatever it was. They chatted and played and laughed. They were dressed in casual clothes. They seemed well cared for and, above all, happy.

As we continued our impromptu inspection, we came across several monks sitting outside a shed peeling vast quantities of pumpkins, onions and other vegetables. There were several open fires with huge pots and a few industrial sized rice steamers behind the shed. Women from a local fishing village were cooking and a lot of youngsters were helping out too, grinding chillies and herbs and adding a selection of local ingredients. We were looking at a village where most of the residents were children.

How had this been achieved? How do the monks manage to feed so many children? Where does the food come from? What about water and clothes? Where does the money come from? My head was buzzing with questions.

Major explained that the monk – U Thu Wona, who was affectionately known as Phongyi – had been handed just one orphan at the height of the wars twenty years ago. Phongyi was himself a young man at the time but adopted the child and had brought him up with the help of a village lady. He'd begun to educate the boy.

More and more children began to arrive and over the following years the monastery with its boarding facilities had become increasingly popular, not just for the high level of formal education provided, but more because of the way their education was uniquely blended with a Buddhist upbringing.

In addition, people from the surrounding towns and villages who couldn't afford to bring up their children were among those seeking places. Phongyi never turned anyone away and before long the monastery was caring for more than five hundred orphaned, abandoned and destitute children.

Life for a child in Burma remains precarious. One in five will die before their fifth birthday. One of the biggest killers is malaria.

Burma has the dubious record of having more than 50 per cent of all malaria-related deaths in South East Asia. Although the majority of the population is rural, most health services are concentrated in urban areas. In 2013 the Government spent less than 4 per cent of its budget on health care compared to 20 per cent on the military. Sanitation and access to clean drinking water remains a prime concern. Much of the underlying blame comes from a lack of education. According to UNICEF only around half the country's children progress to secondary education.

It was against such shocking statistics that this extraordinary monastic haven was able to throw a lifeline to so many children who would surely otherwise have become casualties of this country's fragile environment. Here was a monk, with a handful of saffron-robed helpers, performing nothing short of a miracle.

As I listened to Phongyi, I felt I had stumbled into the midst of something really remarkable, as if he had placed a hand on my shoulder and was about to guide me on a new spiritual path. Where did his inspiration come from? Surely not just from being a Buddhist.

Since my first visit, I had been reading more deeply about Buddhism and its place in Burma. I realised that over the years I had absorbed subconsciously quite a lot of Burmese culture from MuMu and her family. I had learned about the emphasis on confronting life directly and cultivating those qualities that are most central to finding fulfilment as a human being. When we find inspiration, openness and balance within, our lives become genuinely happy and worthwhile. I knew I had been touching on important themes, perhaps understanding them intellectually but not feeling them with my heart. Everyone begins their journey somewhere, I thought. My first uncertain steps began with that meeting by the lake.

CHAPTER 6

LEARNING

'No one saves us but ourselves

No one can and no one may

We ourselves must walk the path'

Buddha

Phongyi was born on the 4 July 1958 in a small village at the foot of the Pa'O mountain range near Loikaw in Shan State, central eastern Burma. There were only five houses. He came from an extremely poor family. His father was a subsistence farmer at the foot of the mountains and the family barely survived.

When he was 15 months old Phongyi's mother died from malaria. He was the youngest child with one sister and an elder adopted son. He missed his mother so much that his father had to console him by pretending to breast feed him. He was too young to be left alone so his father carried him to work on his back. To balance the weight he put some cow dung on one side of the basket. His father soon remarried, but they continued to live in abject poverty and the children were left to fend for themselves.

As soon as Phongyi could walk he was put to work fetching water for the household from the village well some 40 minutes away. He remembers the family being attacked and robbed – even though they had little worth stealing. There was no school nearby so the parents eventually got together to open one themselves. They had no money of their own and the government was not prepared to help because BCP (Burmese Communist Party) insurgents were active in the region. Instead the villagers turned to the PNO leader (the PNO being the political arm of the Pa'O fighters) Aung Kham Hti who helped finance the school and pay for the teachers to take students up as far as the seventh grade.

Classes were constantly disrupted by ideological clashes between the Pa'O and the BCP, and from 1962 on, when General Ne Win had staged his military coup and seized power, both factions were heavily involved in fighting government troops as well. The PNO's national movement to establish an independent Shan State and break the power of the feudal land-owning sawbwas, became a struggle against the military dictatorship.

Unsurprisingly, the school didn't survive for very long, so by the age of fourteen Phongyi was still almost illiterate. The headmaster took pity on him and arranged for him to join the Buddhist monastery at Lin Lam near Loikaw, one of the big towns in that region.

Phongyi would sit all day watching the traffic – the to-ing and fro-ing of bullock carts and traders was in total contrast to his village where people hadn't even seen a house with a tin roof.

'I felt I had to do something to help my people,' he told me. 'It is like the footprint of a cow in a puddle; the frog sits in this little puddle and thinks it's his kingdom. There is a whole world outside but my people did not even know it existed.'

'Go beyond even one's imagination because there is no limit!' he added.

Now I understood one of the secrets of his success. It was a boundless energy and optimism born from a conviction that if you believe something is possible then you can make it happen.

Sam Levenson, the American writer and humourist wrote, ' You have two hands. One is for helping yourself and the other for helping others.'

Phongyi told me how he resolved then that the path to enlightenment for his people was education. He needed to find a way for at least some of the youngsters from the villages around his birthplace to receive a city-based education. But, there was a big problem. Money.

Meanwhile the continued fighting was taking its toll on village life. The PNO had become established politically in 1947 and, over the decades that followed, its military arm of Pa'O fighters had emerged as one of the strongest guerrilla forces in the region. But as it grew it fractured along ideological lines - in 1973 the Communist element within the Pa'O rebranded itself the Red Pa'O and aligned itself with the BCP. This put the original but now much reduced White Pa'O under enormous pressure. They began fighting against each other as well as the BCP and the government forces. To make matters worse the Red Pa'O guerrillas turned to drug trafficking to finance their activities. As a consequence, people living between the Inle Lake and the mountains towards the border with Thailand found themselves in a war zone, sandwiched between the Red Pa'O and the government forces fighting communism.

Somehow Phongyi managed to complete his monastic training, and at the age of 24 settled at the monastery in Lim Lam. The head monk there was a herbalist, so Phongyi's first job was delivering remedies to the various outlying villages. There were no doctors or allopathic medicines at that time, so this service was seen as a lifeline.

The Red Pa'O and other communist parties, notably the BCP, who were still involved in a guerrilla war against the government, relied on the villagers to keep them supplied with food. Villages became isolated and people were too frightened to travel far. They were caught in the crossfire between the government forces, who saw them as spies, and the communists who coerced and often killed anyone who spoke or acted against them. Eventually all the village leaders were appointed by the Red Pa'O. Whole villages were burnt if they were seen to collude with the government.

During all this strife, Phongyi saw his priority as providing safety for the villagers. Wearing his saffron monk's robe gave him a certain protection and influence – and this was something he fully intended to exploit for the good of the community. His mantra was that villagers should remain neutral and not be persuaded or bullied into taking sides – it wasn't their war. If there were to be any discussions they should be conducted outside the village. But he made the mistake of telling the Communists to keep out of the villages and from then on he was branded anti-Communist.

'The BCP told me to leave the village or I would be killed. A mere mortal would have been executed for much less.'

He didn't want to become a martyr before achieving very much, and so he decided to leave the village.

When I asked him more about those times, he admitted that he had thought long and hard about giving up being a monk and taking up arms against the Communists. But in the end he decided it was better to keep to his robes and his teachings and in that way continue to possess influence and also receive donations in order to provide help. Meanwhile, life in the village was becoming horrific. A government informer had been exposed by the BCP, which then proceeded to torture all the other suspected informers. This usually involved pouring boiling oil into the palms of their hands so it would seep right through. Whole villages were burnt and others forced to flee their homes. Four of the village elders were publicly executed as an example to others.

The villagers pleaded with Phongyi to return. He came as soon as it was possible – some two months later, after Vassa, the Buddhist Lent, when he had finished his fasting. He told them not to seek revenge but to remain neutral and go about their own business. He would do his utmost to protect them even if it cost him his life.

The problem was a lack of leadership. No one in the villages was prepared to stand for election because, quite rightly, they knew they would be the first to be singled out by both sides if anything happened. Instead they began to rely more and more on their young monk for everything; if they wanted to build a bridge or a road they would go to him.

Phongyi deduced that if he, with his spiritual calling as a monk, were to appoint the leaders, rather than them being chosen by the government or the BCP, they were more likely to be seen as impartial and trustworthy. Because Buddhists rely on the goodness of the sangha (the Buddhist monastic order, including monks, nuns, and novices) and the practice of non-violence as they follow the path of the dhamma (truth), this turned out to be the right decision. So gradually some sort of normality was restored.

As if to prove the point, on one occasion the BCP threatened that if the villagers didn't help to blow up a bridge used by the government to reach the area, there would be severe repercussions. Phongyi told them they would only do that if the BCP handed in their arms and ammunition. They didn't agree, as you might expect, but at least there were no repercussions. Meanwhile, the Government kept up its pressure on the Communists by establishing a security ring around the villages and cutting off the supplies of food and ammunition. As a result the BCP was severely compromised and the army gradually managed to establish a foothold in the mountain areas, albeit at the price of restricting the freedom of the villagers.

By 1988-89, the Government forces were almost completely in the ascendant, and on the national stage the Communist Party of Burma (the CPB) had more or less collapsed. This fatally weakened the pro-communist ethnic minority militias such as the BCP and the Red Pa'O, who effectively lost their primary source of ideology as well as military support. Consequently, in the Shan Province, both the Red and White Pa'O forces began to observe an informal ceasefire, and the BCP were much reduced as a revolutionary force in local politics.

With the return of some level of safety and stability to the district, Phongyi was once again able to direct his energies towards education and schooling for the villagers. In 1986 he began work on establishing a primary school in Phaya Taung. To raise enough money he had to go to villages much further afield. Persuading them to contribute to another primary school when they were already supporting their own proved extremely difficult. The only way to convince them was by promising to set up a middle school as well. This way he managed to collect four thousand US dollars over a five-year period. It was enough to complete the work on the primary school.

The current development at Phaya Taung began life as a single open-sided building with a roof. Initially there were just sixty children. It took another five years to complete the walls and ancillary building work, brick by brick, and by that time the number of pupils had grown to two hundred. Since most of them came from far and wide, providing boarding places was essential.

The school quickly gained an enviable reputation for its high standard of teaching, and Phongyi, now in his mid-thirties, was elected as head of the twenty-eight school councils in the region. While his role was primarily to supervise the development of the educational programme and ensure the right standards of teaching were being met, people increasingly relied on him for advice and to adjudicate in their disputes, particularly concerning land, domestic and business issues.

I asked Phongyi how he set about deciding on such delicate and sensitive matters. After quietly considering my question he answered in his usual thoughtful manner, which seemed always to balance reason with judicious judgment.

'I didn't make any judgment or ruling. I relied on the 227 scriptures in the Buddhist book of rules as the basis of law. My method was to make the parties understand the futility of being in dispute. Appealing to their better nature, I'd ask them to reach a resolution amongst themselves rather than having an outsider impose a judgment. That way they were likely to resolve their issues without any loss of dignity.'

He gave an example:

'Once there was a fight between two villagers at a festival and one of them beat the weaker person until he was bloodied and injured. The case went to the police magistrates who were likely to award the injured party several million kyats in compensation if the dispute couldn't be resolved between them. After much deliberation I suggested that the aggressor should pay the other person's medical costs and genuinely ask for forgiveness. The man apologised unreservedly in front of all the villagers. The injured party accepted it gracefully and refused to even accept the medical costs.'

Justice had been done with dignity and the two of them became good friends.

COMPASSION

*Living with compassion towards others and developing a sense
of caring helps you manifest inner strength. Kindness and a good
heart form the underlying foundation for success in this life. Once
our hearts are open, all existence appears naturally beautiful and
harmonious. Compassion is the bridge, the spiritual foundation for
peace, harmony and balance. Interdependence is a fundamental law
of nature in Buddhism. By reflecting on the fluctuating nature of
one's relationships with others, and also on the potential that exists
in all sentient beings to be both friends and enemies, it is possible to
develop equanimity and find peace and happiness.*

During his time as a schools counsellor, Phongyi did some research
into the educational standards in each village. His idea was to
ascertain the number of young people who had reached a particular
grade and chosen to remain in their village rather than going off to
the city.

In the district, only one student had passed exams at seventh
grade, at around fifteen or sixteen years old. The following year, the
eighth grade, again just one. And while no one at all had passed
ninth grade, one had passed tenth grade. No one achieved higher
than that.

Realising there was little opportunity for young people to
progress in their own villages, and that all too often those with any
schooling simply moved to the towns and cities, leaving behind

villages filled with uneducated and disadvantaged people, Phongyi set about finding a way to educate the local children until at least the middle grade.

Once again, it was a question of money – in particular finding the fifteen dollars a month to pay the two teachers. More worryingly, there was no money to feed the children. Although the fighting had by now more or less stopped, the villagers were destitute. How was he going to find a way to raise more money?

His solution, or at least part of it, was to open a cinema. At the time very few of the villagers had ever seen a film. Phongyi asked some of his fellow monks in Yangon to buy some Chinese videos, which were readily available, and bring them when they next visited. Using a borrowed video player, a hand-operated generator, and the loudspeaker he usually used for preaching, he set about drumming up an audience.

The school cook doubled as a publicist touring the nearby villages to promote the films. Tickets were five cents per adult, with the same amount for two children. They also sold snacks at the shows. Somehow they managed to raise just enough money to pay the teachers' wages.

But they weren't out of the woods yet, and later when things got really tough they were forced to sell anything they could lay their hands on. Apart from paying the salaries, there was the question of starting a fund for the promised middle school. By now there were over a hundred children in the Primary School, all needing higher education. During the film shows Phongyi lobbied hard for donations to establish a Middle School, promising that the monastery would provide board and lodging, while the parents would have to provide their clothing. This is still the arrangement today.

As I listened to his story, and how the monastery school was begun, I couldn't help but admire his determination. It is difficult enough to raise money in the affluent West, but imagine trying to do this when whole families in Burma are living on less than $200 a year. He also had to convince parents that educating their children would reap rewards – in the form of good jobs that would enable them to send money home. The monastery struggled daily to find accommodation for the children, given the lack of transport and the distances involved. The biggest challenge was to find wages for the extra teachers. Going from house to house with his begging bowl he managed to raise another US $2000. In a nudge toward capitalism Phongyi lent it all to a businessman, charging him interest at $5 a month. This, with the other fundraising efforts including the film shows, provided enough money most months to pay for seven teachers.

The middle school eventually opened on June 17, 1993. This was also the first year the monastery began accepting orphans of the wars and those whose parents could no longer afford to look after them. Up to this point, most of the children had simply been abandoned by parents unable to cope.

During the next fifteen years or so, more and more children arrived as a result of the constant conflicts, disease and poverty. Hundreds of homeless and abandoned children turned up on his doorstep – Phongyi never said no, which is how the monastery also became an orphanage.

To explain just how hand to mouth it was, Phongyi told me that on one occasion they had to sell their only boat to pay the teachers. On another occasion they were forced to borrow money from a local trader to buy fifty bags of rice to feed the children. Just feeding the children became the priority, which meant there was no money for books, pens or paper. Phongyi himself possessed only one robe and a pair of old slippers. They were tough times and it's a wonder the monastery survived.

I remembered when my father in Pakistan had refused to compromise his business by accepting bribes and cutting corners by bulking out his sacks of grain with inferior produce, and how that had led to the collapse of his company and my parents reduced income and living standards. How angry I had been because I suffered. He had continued to give what little he had to street beggars. He once told me, 'When you are charitable you are giving money to God, and he will always repay you more.'

My father's point was that happiness and success come in many different forms, as long as you have belief. His was an inspirational story. I had much to learn if I was to follow in his footsteps.

CHAPTER 7

PLANNING

'I find hope in the darkest of days,

and focus in the brightest.

I do not judge the universe.'

His Holiness the Dalai Lama

By the new millennium the BCP had lost much of its influence and firepower, but despite this the government still regarded the school as being in a separatist area under quasi-rebel control, and continued to deny funding for any projects. Gradually the situation stabilised, and in 2004 the government relented, providing some grants for the school in Samkar as well as for the monastery school at Phaya Taung. They also funded a new hospital, donated a few canoes and built some roads.

At Phaya Taung the old timbered monastery with its sloping verandas and ramshackle collection of roofs and windows was filled to bursting with middle school student boarders and the never-ending new arrivals of children in need. I would have guessed that the original monastery, set on stilts at the edge of the lake, had been built some centuries before, but succeeding generations of monks had added decks and built on rooms as needed. In a way, the building just seemed organic, evolving according to need, and providing spiritual and physical shelter to the monks and villagers over the long years. The dark teak of the wood was timeless, rooted deep into the lakeside soil, ever growing and always sheltering.

With growing numbers of older students, Phongyi turned his attention to extending the middle school, which at that time was in an unprepossessing cement building behind the old wooden monastery, so as to offer improved preparation and instruction for pupils taking high school level exams up to grades nine and ten. The government had rejected his initial approach. It was suggested instead that the children should go to school in Samkar, which was far from ideal because of the distance and travel involved.

The existing staff agreed to extend their teaching to include ninth grade curriculum studies. This still left twenty or so students, studying for tenth grade, who faced the prospect of an arduous journey every day by canoe to Samkar. During the monsoon season this was especially dangerous with the surface water on the lake often whipped up by storms and high winds. Phongyi felt that risking the children's lives in this way was unacceptable, but for the time being there was no alternative. The stress of the journey took its toll, and only one of the children passed their exams.

After that, and for the next few years, the children lodged at various homes in Samkar and the pass rate jumped to 80 per cent. But this wasn't sustainable from a financial point of view. As the number of children studying tenth grade increased, so too did the cost of boarding fees. A way had to be found to enable Phongyi to keep his promise to provide an education leading to a national school exam certificate. Having failed to convince the regional education office in Mandalay, he took his case to the Ministry of Education in the new capital, Naypyidaw.

'I went to pray at the most sacred Buddhist temples in Bagan and Mandalay. I prayed and prayed: God of all beings; parents do not

wish to see their children in trouble; keep them safe, educate and enlighten them.'

I interrupted. Why, I asked, didn't he pray for help to get permission for his school?

'Only God knows if permission for the school is the best outcome for the children,' he said. 'It is best to pray to God for him to provide the best outcome for the children – whatever that might be. Pray with all your heart, mind, body and soul. You should be true to your word and if your prayers are granted you must fulfill the purpose for which you prayed. That is true conviction and faith.'

So why not ask for even more?

'I can only ask what is within my worth to ask. For example, if I ask to become a Buddha I have to have the ways and convictions of a Buddha. That is impossible for the vast majority of us as it requires unimaginable sacrifice and worship: not to walk in case you hurt an ant or a creature of God; to fast without swallowing even your saliva and so on.'

Despite his prayers Phongyi couldn't even get through the front gate. He was stopped and turned away. He kept trying and at his third attempt the guard relented and called the office. He was in.

He was taken to see someone in the schools department dealing with the monastery area. Instead of being faced by blank looks the official knew all about his school and its history and didn't even ask to be shown any records. The official smiled and said he understood the position and would see what he could do. Some months later the Ministry of Education gave its approval enabling a number of organisations to operate schools up to grade ten. There were only three named on the list and Phaya Taung was at the top.

'This was one of the greatest moments of my life. I had fulfilled my promise to all the poor villagers who had put their faith in me and donated money they could ill afford. The future education of our children was now secure.'

By now the monastery was looking after five hundred children of all ages.

Listening to Phongyi, I was struck by his unassuming confidence. He had an aura and presence about him that I found mesmerising. His ability to command such respect, coupled with his calmness and devotion, proved inspirational. How could someone faced with such a herculean task of caring for so many children, with no visible means of financial support, possibly retain such energy and composure? I just knew I was in the presence of someone very special. My own life seemed shallow by comparison. I struggled to be a good father to two children. Here was someone managing to be a good father and teacher to a family of hundreds.

While my own children were growing up I was often too busy worrying about work. I became distant from them and sometimes disengaged from their upbringing and from their feelings too. I could put food on the table and clothes on their backs, but not love in their hearts. You can't buy that – I know that now. Instead of relaxing and enjoying their growing up, I was often irritable. I can see now that it was due to the stress I was feeling, coupled with the constant sense that I needed to impress my clients: all this came at the expense of my family. Without realising it I was mirroring my own upbringing – my life with my own children was a reflection of that. Of course I loved them, as my father loved me, but at the time I never showed it openly. Why should my children have felt any different than I had?

Through the prism of the monastery I became aware of those times in my life that would never return, of my underlying lack of purpose, and I began to question the emptiness I felt. Although I didn't understand it, or indeed appreciate it at the time, the answers were staring me in the face. Everything I needed to know and do was there at Phaya Taung.

The sun emerged through the clouds as Phongyi walked us to the jetty and, as we were about to bid farewell, he asked if there were any suggestions we would like to make to improve the facilities for the children. I had seen the struggle the monks were facing in providing a sanctuary for the children but for some reason the obvious needs of the community went completely out of my mind. There was no time for a considered response. All I could think of was that it would be amazing if the children could be given access to computers.

Phongyi smiled and paused.

'Most of these children have not seen a computer, let alone used one. We don't even have electricity.'

His open question to me had triggered something inside. I thought about everything I had, about the luxuries I took for granted. And then I looked at those children. My inner voice told me I had to do something. I knew I could, and I knew I would. I was unable to sleep that night. I tossed and turned, trying to fathom a way to help those children. Obtaining the computers seemed simple enough, but I would need to overcome the challenge of how to power them given the lack of mains electricity in the village or anywhere in that vicinity. The next morning I started to make local enquiries about how to lay my hands on some generators. Solar charging panels were a possibility, but that seemed more like an option for a bigger power project, so I abandoned that idea.

After searching around on the Internet, I found what I thought would be the perfect solution. Samsung had recently launched a solar-powered computer. I thought it would be worth finding out if they were prepared to donate a few for a very worthy cause which would earn them some good publicity, given the status of Burma as an emerging country. There was likely to be a huge demand for high-tech products there in the future. On my return to London I wrote a formal letter to the CEO of Samsung. I outlined the work of the monastery and asked if the company would consider donating a few of their new solar powered computers to this worthy cause.

I didn't get a reply. So some weeks later I contacted their press office enclosing a copy of my letter and asked if they were prepared to help in any way. I immediately received a short but polite email saying that Samsung could not assist on this occasion.

I was disappointed, but understood their position in that they must receive hundreds of similar requests. However I still needed to get hold of some solar powered computers, and now I was going to have to pay for them. But even that proved impossible because it turned out Samsung didn't sell this type of computer in the UK. I kept getting unhelpful standard computer-generated responses from the contacts provided on the Samsung website, and there were no other telephone numbers listed where I could speak to a real person. I even tried to find suppliers in the US (the equipment was listed on the Samsung US website) but with no success.

I had drawn a blank. Sadly it seemed there was no way that even a paying and willing customer could break through the cyber wall. In the end I turned to my office IT man, who took on the challenge wholeheartedly and came up with an alternative solution. He bought a couple of standard laptops and separate portable solar charging panels specially designed to charge computers and other such portable devices. He also ordered extra laptop batteries and various bits of software to make it all work.

It was now March 2013. I was going to need to return for a fourth time. The best time of year to visit was between November and March but that was just too far away. The rest of the year is either very hot or very wet. May was the earliest I could get away from work, so MuMu and I decided to brave the heat and go then. I emailed asking if we could stay at the monastery for a week or two to teach the children how to use computers. I had also bought some interactive DVDs to help the children with their English, maths and spelling as well as basic computer skills. I included a backup – a selection of Mr. Bean movies, in case we failed with the computer course.

Major promptly confirmed that the monastery would be expecting us, and so we started making preparations for our trip to Inle Lake and in particular to the school and orphanage at Phaya Taung. Our tickets were soon booked and the necessary travel arrangements made. Major said he'd like to stay at the monastery with us, which was a huge relief as we didn't quite know what to expect when we got there.

In the meantime news reports from Burma revealed that the religious tensions between the Muslim Rohingya and the Buddhist Rakhines had erupted into full-blown violence and bloody street battles, undermining further the country's progress towards democracy, and damaging its already fragile international reputation. The fighting had spread from Rakhine State to the region around Mandalay in the centre of the country. There were reports that at least thirty people had been killed in the rioting and of charred bodies lying on the streets of Meiktila, a city not far from Mandalay itself. About six thousand Muslims in Meiktila had been forced to flee their homes and were seeking refuge at a stadium on the outskirts of the city.

The problems largely stemmed from the categorisation by successive governments of the Rohingya tribe, originally from Bangladesh, as illegal immigrants, although many had lived in Burma for generations. To be accepted as citizens they needed to prove they settled prior to 1823 – which given the lack of records was virtually impossible.

On 22 March 2013 the President declared an indefinite state of emergency in four townships in the Mandalay Region – Meiktila, Wundwin, Mahlaing and Thazi. There were even rumours that violence was spreading towards the Muslim areas of Yangon. This was dreadful news, and a serious setback on the country's path to establishing a more liberalised state. Nevertheless the EU announced the lifting of all economic sanctions (though not arms sanctions) and Burma lurched a little further along the rocky road to democracy.

While we waited I used the time to try and decide how best to go about teaching the children. Although I am accustomed to using computers I didn't have the faintest idea how to run classes. What I needed was some inspiration. For now the immediate task was to become familiar with the teaching software, ensure all the equipment was fully charged, and hope that there wouldn't be a problem clearing customs into Myanmar.

We had:

- Two laptops
- Two iPads
- Two solar panels
- Two additional computer batteries
- Two camera /batteries
- An iPod and mobile phones
- Mobile wifi
- Memory sticks
- An assortment of English and maths teaching DVDs plus various other DVDs including Mr. Bean, the Wizard of Oz and Bugs Bunny.

I didn't know Major's whereabouts, or if he was going to be able to join us. I was becoming worried. Finally he emailed to say that, because of his own security (and hence our welfare), he would ask one of MuMu's cousins to escort us to the monastery. He had already made sure our usual boatman would be available.

We bought some Shan clothes – loose baggy pants and shirts for me and longyis or sarongs for us both, and boarded the flight for Yangon on April 25th, still unsure how the trip would work out. Thankfully we had no trouble getting our equipment through customs, and checked in at our usual hotel in Yangon. Major surprised us by turning up with some Pa'O friends, having tracked us down to the hotel bar.

We ordered some cold beers and chatted. At first I thought he might be suspicious of our motives for being there, and wasn't convinced we were serious about the computer classes. Maybe this was why he had been reluctant to accompany us? But after talking for a while he agreed to join us for the remainder of our journey. I was relieved – with Major at our side everything would work out just fine.

Soon we were on the boat heading across the lake for the hotel at Nampan. I felt a real sense of calm, a truly peaceful feeling as though I had returned to where I belonged. I had fallen head over heels in love with this place and its people. While aboard, we had an enjoyable and relaxing last stage to our journey, and I was able to catch up on Major's news. In particular, I wanted to know the rest of his story – what happened after the cattle smuggling?

CHAPTER 8

UNDERSTANDING

'To understand everything
is to forgive everything.'

Buddha

Major had finished his college education in Taungyi, and by the time he was 23 years old had saved enough money from smuggling to enrol into Mandalay University as a maths student. But he continued to make three or four trips a year smuggling livestock into Thailand, using a by now well-rehearsed route. His movements became well known by those manning the Pa'O checkpoints and Major made sure he kept them on-side by always bringing them some presents and spending time drinking and smoking with them. But one day their attitude changed. He was politely detained and taken to see the local commanding officer. The CO was clearly aware of Major's talent for moving goods seamlessly through a string of villages past a number of army checkpoints and across the border without being detected. It was a skill that the Pa'O now wished to exploit. Major's already risky lifestyle was about to become a whole lot more perilous.

The Pa'O wanted Major to become a secret agent. His role would be to recruit and indoctrinate fellow students at Mandalay

University to the Pa'O insurgency. If discovered, such activity would certainly be interpreted as terrorism. Major needed to be both smart and alert. Young students, sympathetic to the Pa'O, who had signed up to the faculty were invited to secret meetings, giving briefings about Pa'O objectives and recruited to the cause. At these meetings Major served up a lethal mixture of alcohol and anti-government propaganda. It did the trick. He quickly established a solid following of students eager to join forces with the rebels. They were deployed in a variety of roles, some in support and some in training camps to become fighters. Major set up a lasting infrastructure at the university where students would continue to be indoctrinated into the Pa'O for years to come. One day he was summoned to the Pa'O command HQ in the jungle.

Among the high-ranking officers he met there was Bo Kyaw, who at the time was the organisation's chief funding officer. Bo was to provide the resources for Major's operations and from then on the two of them worked closely together. It wasn't long before he was promoted to a new role – to set up and formally establish a Pa'O intelligence unit responsible for, amongst other things, organising the safe passage of recruits and personnel to and from Pa'O areas. This was a new non-combatant position and, after some negotiation it was agreed that the position was to bear the rank of major.

The Pa'O had recently reached an agreement with the KNU (Karen National Union) for it to provide military training for their recruits. The KNU was the best organised and the second largest of the minority groups. Being Christians they had joined forces with the British during World War Two and had been well trained by them. In return for support, the British had promised the KNU a separate state, but these regional ambitions were soon overtaken by Burma's troubled post-war history. Major's first task was to arrange safe passage for the first fifty recruits from the Taungyi area to the training camp which was close to the border with Thailand, about two hundred miles away in the state of Kayin – much of it through difficult and dangerous terrain.

On the way a villager warned them that government troops had been stationed in the next town. There was no way round. As they waited Major spotted a Christian funeral procession entering the town. He asked the pastor, whom he had met before, if he would allow his men to join in. The pastor agreed and the men entered the town without being challenged. Arrangements had already been made to house them in return for a donation to church funds and to the village chief. But they were far from being out of danger. The jungle trails were difficult and, although they were armed, they had to be very careful to avoid running into the military patrolling the hills. Major also made sure they avoided any confrontation with the many other tribes and drug gangs that operated along the way. This often meant waving a white flag and negotiating a bribe.

In this way Major and his Pa'O recruits made their way safely through the Kaya state and onwards to Mae Hong Son in Thailand. There they were escorted further south along the border towards Mae Sariang and on to their final destination, the training camp at Minaplaw. He was to make several more of these hazardous trips.

In order to create a credible alias for Major, the Pa'O arranged for him to take up a post as a school teacher at the Patima Mine Pyo monastery school in Nyaung Shwe by Inle Lake. After a few months the Pa'O arranged for an individual of similar age and looks to replace him. It was a clever ruse. To those who knew nothing of this ploy, Major now existed as a schoolteacher. This duplicity allowed him to move around from village to village carrying out his clandestine activities. Now and again he would appear at the monastery to re-establish his credentials.

There was one particular assignment Major remembers well.

Much of his work involved moving men and supplies through the urban areas to the jungle training camps, but he was also busy gathering vital information about the activities and whereabouts of government forces. This assignment involved tracking down a missing Pa'O commander who had been captured by government forces in an ambush on one of their camps near Inle. Commander Aung Tin Oo held far too much information about the Pa'O command structure and identities of undercover operatives for comfort. The military police were well versed in torture techniques which some of their officers had learnt whilst fighting with the Japanese against the British in the Second World War. It was only a matter of time before they would break Aung Tin either by threats to him or his family. So much was at stake that Major was personally assigned to track him down and find a way to either spring him or silence him.

Because Major and the Pa'O enjoyed such local support it was easy enough to discover what the government troops had been up to and if they were still holding Aung Tin in one of the surrounding villages. If that was the case, there was a good chance of finding him. The fear was that he had been moved to a military base in one of the cities. Major had little influence outside the Shan and Kaya areas. Word soon came through that he was being held captive at a military camp in one of the Kaya villages that Major was familiar with as it was on the route to the Pa'O training camp. The village was about twenty-five miles away by jeep. The journey was extremely difficult because he had to travel at night along rough dirt roads avoiding the regular military checkpoints. Eventually he had to abandon the jeep and make his way for the last five miles on foot. This journey had taken all night and by the time Major arrived at the village it was getting light.

From the hilltop overlooking the village he could see the army garrison's makeshift camp in the village school and the surrounding compound. There were some two hundred or so soldiers camped outside and he guessed probably about another hundred in the school buildings – far too many to risk a Pa'O assault. Besides, the military troops were much better equipped than the Pa'O and so fighting their way in wasn't an option.

It was Kason, the second month in the Burmese calendar, which falls between April and May. This is one of the most sacred periods for Buddhists. It is the month of Buddha's birth as well as the month when he attained enlightenment whilst meditating under a Bodhi tree. It is also the month when he died. This most revered of festivals is celebrated nationally, and takes place on the night of the full moon. Offerings are made, and vows renewed, and ceremonies enacted where clean and cool water is poured on and around the Bodhi trees in the communities, in veneration to the Buddha. Major realised that the only people who could gain unfettered – indeed welcome – access to the army barracks would be the monks when they entered as part of their procession. If he could find a way to join their procession it would also give him access to the school compound which was home to one of the oldest Bodhi trees in the village.

So he made his way to the nearby monastery without any real idea how he would persuade the monks to play along with the deception. As he walked into the compound he found the monks were involved in their preparation for the festival. Standing and smiling in front of him was someone Major instantly recognised – it was Ti Hha, the Communist Party escapee who the monks had given refuge to all those years ago. But hadn't he been expelled from the monastery? It transpired that Ti Hha had repented and joined this monastery some years later as a novice, and here he was now a fully-fledged monk. Luckily for Major his revolutionary spirit was undiminished, and he readily agreed to help. He remembered how the young Major had saved his life and tended to him all those years ago. This was at great risk to the monastery's reputation as monks were forbidden from direct political involvement. But Ti Hha was determined to repay Major's kindness.

He gave him one of his saffron robes and helped him shave his head. Ti Hha introduced Major to his colleagues as a monk who was visiting from the Patima Mine Pyo monastery at Inle. Major was already familiar with the protocol of monastic life having served as a monks' helper all those years ago, and so fitting in with the routine for the next three days until the festival started was straightforward. The bigger problem was finding a way of concealing his revolver while dressed as a monk. But he had an idea. He took one of the monks' alms bowls and created a false bottom large enough to hide his ex-British army .38 Smith and Wesson. He covered the revolver in a plastic bag so it was waterproof and placed it in the false bottom of the bowl. Major now had half a plan that would get him into the army camp with his weapon, but then what?

On the day of the festival the monk's procession started with the usual chanting in praise of Buddha with the villagers lining the street or joining in the parade. The monks prayed out loud as the followers stopped to pour water onto the Bodhi trees as they went by.

Finally, the procession reached the barracks where the camp commander welcomed participants into the school compound. On this occasion the public wasn't allowed to enter. The procession reached the Bodhi tree that stood by the side of the school building and the monks began their prayers and blessings with all the soldiers joining in. While they were distracted, Major slipped away unnoticed. He had spotted Aung Tin peering through a window of the school building and so Major began making his way along the corridor in that direction.

As expected, the room was guarded. Major was surprised to see only two soldiers, the others having left to join the ceremony. He moved to greet the soldiers, offering a blessing and putting his hand in the alms bowl and sprinkling water on them. Slightly taken aback, but overawed, they bowed to Major in reverence. He blessed them and moved towards the cell door.

The upper part of the door had been removed and fitted with steel bars so that the guards could keep an eye on their prisoner. Major looked Aung Tin straight in the eye, silently willing him not to show any recognition. After sprinkling some water on the prisoner, Aung Tin asked if he could have a drink from the bowl. The guards, still feeling a sense of privileged elation, agreed and opened the top part of the cell door. Major handed him the bowl.

'Drink from the bowl every day and you will see the light.'

He turned, blessed the soldiers once more, and began to make his way back outside where he rejoined the throng of people.

The next day there was a huge commotion in the camp and sounds of gunfire. Nothing further was heard of Aung Tin Oo.

In 1991 an uneasy peace arrived in the form of a ceasefire agreed by the Pa'O in return for various concessions including land rights and an agreement to start funding education projects again. Many other ethnic tribes made peace at the same time including the Karen, Kayan and some Shan groups. But a few continued their demands for separatist status, notably the Kachin. There were reports of fighting continuing along the Chinese border around Maija Yang. News Agency reports talk of a Kachin army of some ten thousand men armed with antiquated rifles and slingshots fighting a long but losing battle against the government forces.

Effectively, the Kachin were being pushed into China as refugees.

But for the Pa'O the peace agreement was very welcome. It had a profound effect on village life. For the first time in over a generation they were able to lead normal family lives, as men returned from the jungle to resume their previous peaceful occupations. Once again the government began to fund education – building new schools and hospitals and infrastructure projects including much-needed roads and bridges. As well as the obvious benefits, the peace agreement also included provision for members of the Pa'O army to act as a volunteer border force for the government, albeit under the command of the Burmese army.

What really made a difference was the government's initiative in pumping money into funding an employment programme that included support for new business ventures and training. The idea was they would be run as co-operatives, with the workforce recruited from among the Pa'O people, and any profits ploughed back into the community.

Among several such initiatives two in particular are worth mentioning, and they both involved Major. The first had the government leasing some recently discovered ruby mines at Mai Hsu in Shan State to the Pa'O and other ethnic groupings such as the SSA (Shan State Army), the WNA (the Wa National Army) and the KNG (the Kyan National Guard). Given that production at the country's most famous Mogok mines near Mandalay was coming to an end, this was a shrewd move on the part of the government to ensure mining went ahead there and that the operation was profitably run.

Historically, Mogok had been the most important source of rubies. The deposits there had been mined since the fifteenth century. The finest jewellery houses used Mogok rubies because they possessed the most sought after characteristic, a vibrant red colour known as 'pigeon's blood'. Whilst the Mai Hsu mines didn't possess such high quality stones, the deposits were so large that it was hailed as the most important discovery for centuries. The rubies from these mines tended to be lighter in colour with a slightly bluish or purplish hue, which wasn't considered as attractive as the deep uniformly coloured rubies from Mogok. Invariably those from Mai Hsu ended up being heat treated to make them more attractive, but the process also reduced their value. Nevertheless these mines re-established Burma once again as a major source of rubies. The mines provided much-needed employment, but the profits were limited because the stones could only be sold to the government at controlled prices.

Major was appointed operations director at one of the mines. Needless to say he found a way to maximise profits by setting up a lucrative freelance enterprise on the side in which he and his business partner, who put up the money, managed to hive off some of the best stones that they then sold on the black market in Thailand. Major used the money to support the local communities.

The second business opportunity was a brilliant move, but it came at a cost that was not evident at the time. Major had kept in contact with U San Aung (the civil servant who initiated the peace deal). On one occasion when Major and U San were admiring the beauty of the lake, U San had said how amazing it would be if travellers were able to visit and stay there. Therein were sown the seeds of the idea to build the first hotel on the lake. U San had a friend, Kenny McLennan, a Scottish architect, who visited Burma on a regular basis.

On one such visit U San and Major asked him about the possibilities of designing and building a hotel and whether he was prepared to undertake the project. Kenny agreed and Major put the plans to the Pa'O council for approval. After much deliberation they were approved, but at half the size originally proposed.

Major was appointed the building director. The inspiration for the design came from the local Intha village huts that were constructed from bamboo and woven straw. There were many obstacles to be overcome; the biggest being the lack of electricity and drinking water, which continue to be a problem to this day.

Funding the project and sourcing the right materials was also a huge headache. The government provided a modest grant, which helped pay for some of the fixtures and fittings needed, but finding the raw materials for the actual construction was a different matter altogether.

Major embarked on a fundraising roadshow, going from village to village securing pledges for bamboo and other building materials. Where families couldn't afford to donate materials they invariably offered their services as labourers. Then, before even half the structure had been completed, Kenny McLennan died. That's when cousin Ting stepped in and finished off the project. The hotel opened for business in 1996.

As promised, the very first dividend to the local Pa'O community came in the form of jobs at the hotel. Major had already earmarked some of the smartest and brightest locals from the nearby villages, but they still needed training. There were two basic roles to be filled: general hotel staff and entertainers. Finding locals who could provide first-class service was easy because their Buddhist upbringing ensured they were naturally polite and mild-mannered. The second requirement was the ability to entertain guests, which meant a willingness as well as an ability to sing, dance, or play some form of musical instrument. So began a tradition, that remains to this day, where every evening the staff put on a dance and music show at dinner – moving seamlessly between cooking, serving and performing on stage.

This very first hotel provided the impetus for a tourist boom at Inle Lake, which has since become one of the country's top holiday destinations. More than two million tourists visited Burma in 2014 and many of them included a trip to Inle Lake. There are now several luxury hotels and spa resorts in the area but demand still far outstrips supply, especially in the peak season between November and March when it is essential to book many months ahead to guarantee somewhere to stay.

The next afternoon, while we were staying at the hotel at Nampan, Major, Ting, Sabai and cousin Lette arrived to make plans for our stay. Ting and Bo said they wanted to show me a modern day catastrophe that would change the face of the lake and the community forever. Bo had been restoring his jeep, which dated from the Second World War, and the boys piled in with Bo driving and Major in the front passenger seat. Both men were wearing US army caps while Bo also had a pair of binoculars around his neck. I imagined them looking exactly like this in their military days.

Bo drove up the east side of the lake and it wasn't long before we all had a good view of what was happening. It was sheer devastation. The entire base and one side of the mountain had been bulldozed and flattened for development. Bo explained how enough land was being sold to build a hundred new hotels with a capacity of more than five thousand rooms. The current capacity of five hundred rooms already placed a strain on the fast dying lake and this looked as if it could be its death warrant.

Dramatic measures were going to be needed to ensure that the river system and springs that feed the lake didn't become polluted with pesticides and other chemicals. I read in the local papers that the UN had offered to help preserve and restore the polluted areas of the lake but that local politics were getting in the way of it happening.

It was a difficult and sensitive issue for the local Intha and the Pa'O. Whilst not wanting to stand in the way of progress, which would boost tourism and thus their standard of living, they were also wary of any development that would ruin the very thing the tourists came to see. Unless the construction was undertaken in an environmentally sensitive manner, and with due respect to the local people, it would be disastrous.

Perched on the top of the hill, Bo and Major shared the binoculars as they surveyed the area, pointing here and there while discussing how best to lobby politicians to save their beloved lake. At least this crude invasion of concrete couldn't take away the beautiful golden sunset that was, paradoxically, enhanced by the dust from the excavations. It turned the light into a hazy dark red glow. Perhaps the sun was expressing its own anger. That evening Bo organised another dinner party, which was accompanied by more whisky and a bottle of local sauvignon blanc, but it was hard to get into the spirit of the occasion after what we had just seen. As I looked across the ravaged landscape by the lake that evening, I felt some sadness at the prospect of what I saw in front of me. The PNO needed to adopt a different approach to this battle, using negotiation and diplomacy rather than the gun. I wondered whether these former guerrillas were armed with the right credentials to fight this type of battle in the political minefields of Naypyidaw, the country's new capital.

IMPERMANENCE

Everything by nature constantly changes. I had been learning that insight into impermanence is central to Buddhist practice. Everything is subject to change and alteration. We need to accept that existence is both a precious moment, and a continuous becoming.

According to the teachings of the Buddha, life is comparable to a river. It is a progression, a successive series of different moments, joining together to give the impression of one continuous flow. All that is real is the present, and that itself is a product of the past. Impermanence and change are the undeniable truths of our existence.

'All conditioned things are impermanent –
when one sees this with wisdom, one turns away from suffering.'

Buddha

CHAPTER 9

TEACHING

'He is able

who thinks he is able.'

Buddha

E arly the following morning we set off for the monastery. I was full of conflicting emotions and some trepidation too. Were we doing the right thing by introducing computers – would it destroy the natural harmony of their village lives? Were we just another lot of rich westerners promising to make a difference? Were we really welcome? I so wanted to help but I knew there was often a trade-off to be had between learning new skills and the frustration of finding nowhere to go.

From the hotel in Nampan to the monastery is about seventy kilometers, and we travelled in two boats for the journey as Ting, Sabai and Bo all wanted to see us settled in. Knowing we were going to be on a vegetarian diet for the next week or so, we took with us cartons of juice and protein bars.

The water levels at some parts of the lake were very low following the dry summer season. Only the skill of our boatman, with an occasional helping hand from the young boys swimming alongside, enabled us to get through. After about three hours we stopped at

Samkar before heading for the monastery. Within minutes we were surrounded by food and more food – bowls of rice, cooked vegetables, different savoury snacks and of course green tea. We were joined by what must have been the village leaders. This was no ordinary welcome. I worked out that it was because Bo Kyaw was with us. The villagers had been complaining about the lake weed, which was choking the area and making it impossible for them to use their boats. Bo had intervened on their behalf, lobbying the local authority through the PNO to clear the growth. Now the villagers wanted to thank him. Needless to say there were clearly other issues to resolve and Bo listened attentively.

While we were there, and as we were passing a number of ancient stupas (Buddhist shrines), Ting took me by the hand and showed me how these monuments were being destroyed. They were being ruined not by the ravages of time and natural erosion, but by the obsessive and yet insensitive manner in which the local people were trying to restore them. This involved covering them in cement and applying cheap gold paint, believing this would please their God and guarantee them a better incarnation in the next life.

He showed me a six hundred-year-old stupa that he had lovingly restored with the help of local craftsmen. It included decoratively painted walls and ceilings, full of symbolism, and a beautifully restored teak roof. He had pleaded with the local people to look after it, but he realised he was fighting a losing battle. In their view, matching Ting's standards of quality work wouldn't earn them the rewards that an instant covering of cement and cheap paint would.

Then it was time for lunch and more food. We were taken to a new restaurant owned by Bo's niece who had married into the infamous family responsible for producing the rice wine – and many headaches. The young couple had been told to expect us, and we enjoyed an enormous feast that was particularly welcome given the fairly basic rations we could expect at the monastery. We took the opportunity to wash it down with more of the rice wine, knowing we were definitely going to be deprived of alcohol for the next few weeks.

After lunch we headed straight for the monastery at Phaya Taung, which was still another hour away. The lake here was wide, deep and crystal clear – a complete contrast to the northern part, which was rapidly becoming overdeveloped. Our small craft struggled through the waves, spraying water all over us. But we were all well equipped with umbrellas and waterproof jackets. We held the umbrellas horizontally in front of us to protect our legs from getting soaked. This was certainly no pleasure cruise.

There was a complete absence of activity on this part of the lake except for thousands of wild birds feeding in the fields bordering the banks. At that moment, I seemed to be living in two universes, immersed in nature's unfolding drama on the lake, and at the same time apprehensive about our teaching week ahead in the monastery. With no computer teaching experience and virtually no understanding of the language, I was beginning to feel we would need a great deal of luck and help to make this trip a success. As the boat lurched onwards, I prayed for further inspiration.

After a slow and difficult journey and a good soaking we finally got to Phaya Taung. Just as we arrived an idea came into my head.

We were greeted by Oo Pazin, the deputy head monk, and some teenage students who helped carry our bags and computers up to the monastery. As we walked up the track from the jetty, we got a glimpse of what life here was really about. Sitting under a large red blossom tree was a little boy perhaps five years old. He was wearing an old blue T-shirt and a pair of dirty shorts and was completely engrossed in eating a bag of sweets. He was clutching it desperately as if his life depended on it, and he was oblivious to our presence.

Somehow he seemed out of place in the calm and supportive atmosphere of the monastery. Oo Pazin said something to him as we passed, but he didn't even look up. He was totally preoccupied and, on closer inspection, clearly very agitated. I sensed Oo Pazin saw both disapproval and surprise in our eyes.

He broke into a smile and then laughed, which broke the spell. I was relieved – I confess I had been thinking that I might have been mistaken about the monastery. In a situation like this at home, I would have expected Oo Pazin to reprimand the child for eating sweets and ignoring us. I wondered a little about the teaching and the discipline in the school. I needn't have – the loving kindness of the monks towards the damaged victims of the wars soon became clear to me when I learned more about their care and deep compassion. I had been wrong-footed by my own ill-considered prejudices, and I recognized then that I had at least as much to learn as to teach in this place.

He explained how the boy had arrived only two days ago and how he was thought to be from the Lisu mountain tribe because he didn't speak a language they understood. He was probably an orphan – or abandoned. And because he didn't have a name they called him Mayawk, which means monkey. He was completely traumatised. The monks had adopted him and were trying to win his confidence by giving him anything he wanted. But all he appeared to want were the sweets he had spotted in the local village shop.

I didn't ask Oo Pazin what had happened to his parents; instead I asked Major a few days later. He told me how hundreds of desperate young people had been illegally making their way across the border into Thailand as economic migrants. Completely unaware of the dangers of sexual disease, too many of them had contracted AIDS. Destitute illegal immigrants have no access to medical facilities, and when they return to their own villages, often seriously ill, they don't get proper medical help there either. The result is that many of them die.

We were led to the monastery where Phongyi made us all feel at home. Bo, Major, Ting, Lette, MuMu and I sat around in a semicircle. We were served the ubiquitous green tea with delicious pieces of tofu kyaw. I was keen to get going on setting up our project, but Major signaled me to hold back and wait until the right moment. I had learned by now that the monastery's teaching and care work was to a certain basic extent supported by the PNO, the political, cultural and welfare arm of the Pa'O people in Shan Province, and that Bo and Phongyi enjoyed a close working relationship. The fact that Bo was with us was a clear endorsement of our good intentions.

I felt the right moment had come to broach the subject of our role. Through Major, I asked Phongyi if he had any particular ideas or instructions about how he wanted us to conduct the classes. He said he was happy to leave that to us. We had brought two laptops from London and acquired access to two secondhand ones locally, so I suggested that we taught the children in classes of around eight at a time. We would start with the ten-year-olds for two hours in the morning and two hours in the afternoon. I felt the younger ones were likely to pick up the basics faster than the older ones. Eventually, all being well, the youngsters could become the teachers.

Phongyi liked that idea, but suggested we also taught the older students who were between eighteen and twenty, because they were likely to stay on either in their villages or at the monastery as teachers. He thought we could begin at eight am and finish at six, which meant we could also fit in a two-hour class for the other children in the morning and afternoon. It would be a full timetable for us all.

He realised we must be tired, but before we could rest Phongyi wanted to show us the school and the classroom we would be using. Clustered around the old wooden monastery were a number of single storey buildings made of concrete and timber, with two classrooms each. These had been simply but effectively designed to accommodate the ever-increasing numbers of children in classes ranging from 5 years old all the way up to tenth grade at 16-18 years old. I could see that the dignified but ageing teak-built monastery was no longer really used primarily as a place of prayer and meditation – all the resources of the community had been put to use to house the overwhelming number of children arriving at Phaya Taung. Some of the buildings doubled as classrooms during the day and dormitories or eating areas at night.

We were shown the room set aside for our classes. It was spacious with a white board, a row of tables and twenty or so chairs. On either side of the desks was a row of about a dozen keyboards along with some empty boxes stacked in a cupboard. These had been recently donated, and they were the extent of the school's IT equipment. What the room lacked in sophistication it made up for it with a distractingly beautiful view of the lake. We felt honoured to be assigned one of the best available spaces for our teaching.

It was now late afternoon and time to bid farewell to our escort party. I am not sure why, but they seemed very quiet amongst themselves as we walked them to the jetty. On reflection I think it was because they were worried we might find it difficult to adapt to our rigorous teaching programme, and the crowded surroundings far from the comforts of the hotel.

Our living quarters were in a building at the far end of the monastery. Downstairs was an open basement area where all the food and other supplies were kept. On the ground floor, where we entered, was a longish room some fifteen by thirty feet, which was used as a dormitory during the night and a dining area during the day. It contained a table, several plastic chairs and not much else.

An area about six feet by twelve had been partitioned off for us. This was where we would be sleeping. Our beds comprised a double blanket laid out on the floor. We were really fortunate that Major had arranged to bring us fresh towels and a clean white sheet. But the real lifesaver was the mosquito net that our boatman rigged up around our sleeping area. This would protect us not only from the ever-present mosquitoes, but also from all sorts of insects and creepy crawlies, particularly lizards.

At the other end of the room was a similar space that Major would share with the boatman and one or two students. There was one Western-style toilet. The shower consisted of a hosepipe that led to the balcony for all of us to use. Having got used to our surroundings, and explored a little, we realised that this was real luxury. Unsurprisingly, there was very little in the way of washing facilities at the monastery – the boys mainly used the lake, and the girls had access to a few toilets and a communal bathing area.

We left our bags in our room and made our way to the classroom where we carefully set up the computers, solar panels, and additional batteries and generally got a feel for the place, mentally preparing ourselves for the next day. I felt pretty good about the computers, and keen to start the teaching sessions we had planned. I paused to take stock, as the anticipation of what the next week would bring continued to build. We had managed to transport the computers and equipment all the way from London to Yangon, and then up to Inle Lake, through customs and past occasional checkpoints, without loss or delay. I felt it was an auspicious start.

As we walked towards our living quarters, the deputy head monk Oo Pazin approached and asked if we were comfortable. He then pointed us in the direction of a magnificent old Bodhi tree, on the side of which stood an open shelter. As it was a beautiful evening he suggested having our dinner there with Major and the boatman.

And so began our daily routine. Four or five smiling young girls would appear, chat to MuMu in Burmese and serve our dinner. Three times a day for the next seven days this was more or less the same meal: rice, a watery vegetable curry, a cooked vegetable dish, and some pickled fruit or vegetables such as green mango, mustard leaves or edible flower buds. There was always a plentiful supply of green tea and bananas. Sometimes we were served fried peanuts as a source of protein.

I discovered later that, except on special occasions, the children had to be content with just rice and the watery vegetable curry; the other food was reserved for the special guests. Oo Pazin said the girls who were waiting on us would attend our first class the following day. This gave us the opportunity to get to know each other. It was a quietly happy evening and I felt genuinely at peace in the midst of this kindness and hospitality. Oo Pazin bid us good night, saying breakfast would be served at six.

We were exhausted from the journey, and the excitement and anticipation, so we slept well, oblivious to the insects and lizards sharing our sleeping quarters. From that night on we began to get accustomed to living with the creatures around us. Often I would find a lizard or two peering at me through the bed sheets as I woke. But we never got used to the mosquitoes.

Life at the monastery began with the monks rising at four am for meditation and prayers. We awoke around five as the sun began streaming into our room. The sounds of the monastery's gentle comings and goings could be heard intermingled with birdsong and the noise of various domestic animals. I realised that we were in a very remote place that until twenty years ago had been a jungle where tigers and other wild animals roamed. Nature's choir was telling us that morning had broken.

We quickly showered and dressed, but the children were already in front of us. They were chatting excitedly on the steps outside the building's entrance, peering in occasionally to see if we were about to begin. Soon we were joined by Major. The three of us were served a hearty breakfast, but we could barely manage a mouthful. We were excited, but in a nervous way. What we really needed was a cup of that strong local coffee we were used to back at the hotel. We knew the children would have high expectations and we didn't want to disappoint them.

Slightly ahead of schedule we went to the classroom, where we were soon joined by four novices, all boys, and four girls – all somewhere between eight and ten years old. Then Phongyi, Oo Pazin and several other adult teachers came in and sat at the back of the room, watching and waiting for us to perform miracles. The children gathered at their desks, two to each computer, fiddling with the keyboards and waiting impatiently to get started. This was it. No turning back now. It was time for my master plan.

MuMu – my talented artist, photographer, translator, guide and long-suffering wife – began by drawing a large house on the whiteboard. She followed my instructions and drew a gated entrance, a lock on the door, and several rooms with filing cabinets. She had no idea what I was attempting to reproduce here but thankfully she had enough faith in me to keep going. When she had finished the drawing I told the children, as translated by MuMu, that they were about to enter a magnificent English country house. To get into it they would have to switch on the computer (press the start button), walk towards the door and open it with the key (password), and enter. They could go into any room: the maths room (Excel) or the English library (Word), the drawing room (Paint) or the mail room (Outlook). They could open a cupboard (the Software programme) and, having made use of the contents, they could keep them by storing them (Save) in a filing cabinet (Folder).

The children grasped the concept immediately and it helped them find their way around the computer's functions effortlessly. Using the mouse was a little awkward at first but they soon got the hang of it after a bit of guidance and practice. By the end of the session they all knew how to start the computers, access the programmes, and close them down properly. Oo Pazin, who was in charge of education overall at the monastery, was enthusiastic about my concept of a magical house. During the afternoon session we introduced the children to the various DVDs so they could work on their own and practice using the mouse.

The same approach worked equally well for the older children, so at this point I realised we only needed one syllabus, which I drew up along the following lines:

Day 1: Introduction

Day 2: Word

Day 3: Excel

Day 4: Paint

Day 5: Outlook (and merge Excel / Word/ Paint)

Day 6: Presentation by the students

Day 7: Closing session.

MuMu used the time to teach the children how to type, as there was an abundant supply of redundant keyboards. The younger children enjoyed the DVDs on maths, English and spelling exercises, whilst the older children were more interested in honing their practical work-related skills, such as preparing CVs or producing budgets for fledgling businesses. All-in-all, the younger group got a handle on things faster than the older ones. One particular eleven-year-old novice had completed much of the course and was proficient in all the Microsoft office programmes within two and half days. As the course gained momentum, more and more people joined in as observers, and often the other teachers came and helped – learning

in the process. Visiting relatives peered through the windows in astonishment at what their children were doing. So, from a class of eight with two to a computer, we progressed to three sharing each workstation, enthusiastically supported by a group of onlookers and helpers joining in. On each occasion we would have between fifteen and twenty people in the room. The lessons took on a life of their own.

The children were so keen that we hardly had time for lunch and rarely finished before seven. They either arrived early or stayed late practicing – that's if they were lucky enough to get their hands on a computer or the batteries hadn't run out by then. What was truly remarkable about the children was not their aptitude or gratitude or even their keenness to learn, but the manner in which they conducted themselves. They showed us how dignified and courteous they were, and how caring and considerate to one another, always willing to share and ensure everyone got a fair go.

We started befriending one cautiously inquisitive visitor. Mayawk (the monkey) came to watch us through the window, but persisted in asking Oo Pazin for money to buy sweets. MuMu asked Oo Pazin why he pandered to Mayawk's constant demands for sweets and why he, and indeed everyone else including the other children, indulged Mayawk's every demand. Oo Pazin explained the monastery culture.

'Mayawk is very vulnerable and his greatest need is all the kindness we can offer. We don't want him to learn how to shout or get angry – this is not our way. Soon, but only when he is ready, we will move on to rewarding him only when he has completed his tasks.'

The monk felt that in the fullness of time he would adopt the kindness and consideration shown by the other children. But for now it was all about winning his confidence. Never a word was spoken to him in anger or rebuke. By the end of our stay we had

already begun to see some remarkable changes in his behaviour. He began to communicate and understand Pa'O; he would smile and was clearly much happier; but he still kept up his demand for sweets, although now he was prepared to wait for them. He stopped peering through the window of our classroom and instead would come into the room. He took a particular interest in my iPad rather than the PCs – clearly this was a boy with an eye on the future.

Generally, the children began to enjoy the lessons more and more as they learned their way around the computers. Often they would be waiting for us outside the classroom with songs of appreciation and high fives. We were carried along by their enthusiasm.

One of the exercises we asked each student to complete was to write an essay about their life and experience at the monastery. Here is one of the children's stories, exactly as it was written down for us. I discovered during the teaching sessions that they could write English far better than speak it – that would come with practice.

'My name is Ma May Than Nu. I live in Pha Yar Taung. I reached here at 2004. This village has many wonderful places. In this village all the people are very kind and help good relationship with me. My grandfather's name is U Sam Mya and my father's name is U Maung Than. He is a farmer. I have made many friends when I reached in Pha Yar Taung. Among them, my best of my friend is Ma Saw Myint and she is very kind and relationship. She is a fatherless child and a poor girl. She always helps many people.'

May Than Nu was born in the village of Hti Wa Mu in Nyaung Shwe Township, which is at the very northern end of the lake. Her grandfather was a member of the Lisu tribe, but joined the Pa'O insurgents and became a fellow freedom fighter with Major. He was wounded during the fighting and had to have steel rods inserted in one of his knees. As a result, he had difficulty walking and eventually died from an infection. Her father was a farmer in a small village with a population of about a hundred. There were six children. Three of her younger sisters had died; one from malaria when she was just two, the others in a fire at home. May Than Nu survived because she and her mother were visiting an aunt in another village at the time. The tragedy tore her family apart. Eight years ago May Than Nu was handed over to the monks in the hope they could help rebuild her life and provide her with a better future. She had recently passed her exams and was hoping to train as a nurse – an ambition May Than Nu was to realize fully in Yangon later on.

May Than Nu's story was typical of many of the children here. Others had seen their parents killed in the fighting, or simply been so poor they couldn't afford to feed their children. In many cases the mothers had died in childbirth and the fathers had been killed in the wars. In Burma the average household needs to spend 70 per cent of its income on food compared to 57 per cent in Bangladesh, which is seen as one of their poorest neighbours. In Thailand, the figure is just 32 per cent.

The days flew by, as we were always so busy. On a couple of occasions I escaped for a walk around the local village with Oo Pazin, but even that was always quite rushed as the girls were already waiting to serve us dinner. As soon as we had finished eating, Phongyi would join us and we would talk late into the night, which meant we were exhausted by the time we went to bed.

During one such evening conversation, we were discussing the course and exchanging views on the children's progress. At this time, we had only four working computers, and we were teaching up to twenty students in rotation. We divided them into two groups: the first group was made up of students between 9-11 years old, enabling us to discover how quickly the younger children would pick up computer skills, even though at that time they had never even seen a computer. The second group comprised the 18-20 year olds, and here we wanted to identify students who might stay on after the course and help teach.

By far the most accomplished was an eleven-year- old called San Aung. Never having even opened a computer before, he was working through Microsoft Office programmes on day two, and after less than ten hours of tuition was becoming expert. When I introduced him to the Paint programme, he became equally proficient in no time at all. He was brilliant at everything he did. So naturally talented was he that Phongyi thought he could become the country's next President.

'He is a truly remarkable boy, well ahead of the others.'

Apparently, San Aung's parents divorced when he was about three. He went to live with his father while his little brother stayed with his mother. But his father abandoned him, and he ended up being taken in by the monastery. Now he was training as a novice monk. About five years ago when he was eight he had asked to see his mother again. The monks managed to trace her and arranged a visit. After a few days San Aung returned to the monastery and asked to bring his younger brother. Phongyi said he could, but only if his mother came too.

I did not understand the full significance of that until Phongyi told me a story.

'Once upon a time a young man saw a very handsome monk having a bath and thought to himself that if I were a woman I would really marry this man. The power of the monk made this man's wish come true and he became a woman. But since he was already a married man with children, he could not return home as a woman. So he disappeared from his family. They thought that he was dead.
He began to live like a woman and one day she met a woodcutter.
They fell in love and the woodcutter took her to his village and they

got married and had children. Some years later some villagers from where she had once lived visited the woodcutter's village and she recognised one of them, so she asked about her family. The visitors were surprised when she told them that she was asking about her wife and children. So she explained that she had once been a man, and even the woodcutter did not know about her past, but now she desperately missed her old family. The visitors told her she should go to this handsome monk and ask for his forgiveness. She found the monk and asked for forgiveness and so she became a man again. Lots of people asked him what it was like to be both a mother and a father. He said that a mother carries her child for nine months, nurses and looks after the child. There is simply no comparison between the love of a father and the love of a mother for a child. But equally, while there is a unique bond between a mother and child, in our teaching everyone is your mother and your father.

The course ended with a presentation by all of the students. The idea was that each of the older students would pass on the skills they'd learned to the younger ones. This turned out to be very impressive – at least four of them had real teaching potential. We thought we were at the stage where the ability of the students and their eagerness to learn computing could form part of their curriculum. It would certainly help them find jobs and at the very least equip them for the future, which even in Burma was becoming dependent on technology. We now needed to get hold of another ten or twenty computers in order that every child would have the chance to learn.

At the end of the course, Major presented all the students with awards. The only things we could buy at the local shop, which was half-an-hour away by boat, that would make suitable prizes, were torches for the boys (there was no electricity) and sarongs for the girls. MuMu organised a special bag of goodies for Mayawk – not more sweets, but a set of clothes, some shoes and basic school essentials including pencils and erasers. This was his passport to attend the classes.

Phongyi thanked us before asking me to address the students. I wasn't prepared for that, but I did my best to improvise. I said that a human being learns all the time and sometimes the young teach the old. The students had learned some computer skills from us. But we had learned a lot more from them. We had seen them behave with humility, kindness, generosity, and with utmost dignity at all times. We should aspire to learn how to live by their example.

These were lessons we could apply to our often chaotic and stressful way of life back home.

Forget safety. Live where you fear to live.

Rumi

R E N E W A L

I began to realize that it was only fear that was holding me back from making important changes to my life. By discarding fear, I could hit the re-set button and move more completely towards living a life of purpose, contribution and commitment. I was discovering that I wasn't so separate and distinct from others. The children at the monastery were teaching me that the more we take the welfare of others to heart and work for their benefit, the more benefit we attain for ourselves. I was beginning to listen to my heart and find the path of openness and compassion. It is in the heart centre that our inner nature grows to fullness, and here there is no distinction between compassion and wisdom.

CHAPTER 10

BELIEVING

'Just as treasures are uncovered from the earth,
so virtue appears from good deeds
and wisdom appears from a pure and peaceful mind.'

Buddha

During one of our late night talks, while Phongyi told me about his life and work, I asked his advice about how best to deal with issues in my personal life. I was troubled by my own inability to deal with certain situations. Pressures of work meant I sometimes became stressed at home. I wanted to learn from this man and become not just a better person, but a wiser one too. I am a bit of a perfectionist – I like things to be ordered – and this probably makes me difficult to live with. At times, I might be rather diffident and appear a little cold or distant towards my children. I could be strict without realising the impact I was having on them. This was my opportunity to explore some of these issues.

MANAGING ANGER

I began by asking how it was that the monastery seemed so calm and serene. It ran like clockwork with never a word spoken loudly, let alone in anger. How did he achieve that and what were the lessons in running a community or building a business?

'In my sermon every day I give the same guidance: you have the freedom to say anything, but never make another unhappy by what you say and by what you do. I tell them to think clearly, speak clearly and do their job clearly.'

What if the job doesn't get done?

'If they complete their duties their job is done. If they do more than their duties, it is praiseworthy.'

But what if they still do not finish them?

'Speak to them without anger. Anger breeds more anger. If they still do not fulfil their duties, you should repeat what you have already said. If their actions do not change they are asked to go back to their village and to their own fate.'

In a work setting, which is usually a stressful environment, surely controlling anger is more easily said than done?

'Anger is the product of greed. To control your anger you need to keep in check your greed. You make mistakes when you are angry and this makes the other person unhappy. You set a bad example because you create a culture of blame. Practise forgiveness. We all make mistakes.

'Do not be greedy and you will control your anger. Your working life will be peaceful, you will prosper, so will your family and all who are around you.'

FINDING SUCCESS

What attributes are required to succeed in your work, or indeed in any endeavour? What part does hard work or luck play in its success or otherwise?

'If you want to succeed, you need to use all your God-given faculties and at the same time make your own luck.'

He outlined his recipe for success:
- *Vision – Visualise your final goal.*
- *Heart – Make your commitment.*
- *Mind – Think through your options on how to get there. Choose intelligently.*
- *Work – Be smart and work hard; patiently build a strong foundation one brick at a time.*
- *Luck – Make your own luck by doing good deeds.*

Phongyi illustrated his teachings with stories or, more precisely, with Buddhist allegories to help us understand better:

There are two friends. The first one believes in doing good deeds to make his luck. The second one believes in destiny. One day the two friends are travelling through a forest and a storm overtakes them.

The first one, who believes in doing good deeds, is hit by falling fruit. The second, who believes in fate, is nearly hit by a falling tree under which he finds a pot of gold.

So the second friend said to the first – I am luckier than you because it was my fate to find the pot of gold and in spite of your good deeds you only got a handful of fruit.

They went to the astrologer who told them that the first friend was meant to have been struck by a bolt of lightning but he was saved by his good deeds. The second friend was actually meant to have become a king – he was unlucky to have only found a pot of gold.

He concluded:
You can change your destiny by good deeds but the consequence of your actions is something you will not always know.

PRACTISING KINDNESS AND SELF PRESERVATION

In work as in life you come across many different types of people. If you don't get on with someone, or find them difficult to work with, how do you resolve this?

A man is travelling from one town to another through the jungle. He gets lost on his way and falls into a deep ditch. A large monkey who has been watching sees him trying to get out. The man is desperate to escape before nightfall, fearing that otherwise some wild animal will kill him. The monkey says to the man: 'I will carry you on my back and I will leap out. But just to make sure that you don't get hurt let me practice first with some heavy stones.'

The monkey does this successfully several times and so asks the man to get on his back. He jumps out safely.

The monkey is very tired and says to the man: 'Let me sleep in your lap for a little while to rest.'

The man watches the monkey go to sleep and thinks that he has nothing to bring back to his wife – why not kill this monkey? The

*meat will be a good present to take her. He takes a stone and hits
the monkey on the head but the monkey jumps up bleeding from the
wound, and escapes up a tree. The monkey says: 'I was kind to you
and rescued you and now you are trying to kill me?'*

*The man tries to find his way home but goes round in circles
becoming lost, hungry and tired. The monkey takes pity on him and
throws him some fruit. He sees he will die in the jungle unless he finds
his way home. So the monkey tells the man: 'I will show you the way
out as I move from tree to tree but I will not come down. Follow the
drops of my dripping blood and they will lead you home.' The man
follows the monkey and reaches home safely.*

Phongyi added:

*So you see, you can always do business and be kind and courteous
even if this is not reciprocated. Human beings are imperfect, and yet
we are interdependent on one another. Consequently it is important
to understand fully the other person's shortcomings and weaknesses
and be prepared to act in such a way so as to avoid any harm coming
to oneself.*

'Know your enemy and know yourself
and you can fight a hundred battles without disaster.'

Sun Tzu

THINKING ABOUT DEATH

Thousands have lost their lives in the numerous uprisings. How did you console the bereaved families – especially when it involved the loss of a child?

'Once there was a very rich old man who had lots of gold and silver but overnight it all turned into coal. He asked the village elder what happened and was told that his luck had run out. The village elder told him to go to the market and sell all his coal.

Everybody in the market made fun of him; this rich man selling coal. But a very beautiful woman saw that he is really selling gold. The man says to the beautiful woman, 'I will give you jewels if you marry my son.' So she does and the coal turns back into gold.

His son and his beautiful wife are very happy together and have a lovely baby boy who is the apple of their eye. The old man feels that his luck is changing. But one day the baby boy dies. The old man with his grandchild in his arms runs around desperately to the palmist, the clairvoyant, the herbalist and says to them that he will give all his gold to anyone who can give back his grandchild's life; they cannot. He reaches the temple and asks the monk. The monk tells him that only the Buddha can give him life and points him to a man sitting in the corner of his monastery.

The old man goes to the Buddha and in desperation asks if he will give life to his grandchild. The Buddha says that he can only restore his life if the old man can find at least one household that has mustard oil and where they can also say that there has been no death in their family. The old man runs from house to house. Most offer him mustard oil but none can confirm that there has been no death in their household.

He realises that luck can restore material wealth but nothing can bring back life. He buries his grandchild and accepts that in everyone's life there is death.

In Buddhism we are punished in this life for our misdeeds from this or a previous life. But you can negate your past misdeeds by doing good deeds in this life.

As if to reinforce this, Phongyi continued:

There is a story about a holy man who was close to the Buddha. He was a gifted man who could see and hear everything, the past as well as the future, and he could read everyone's mind.

One day, an enemy put a high price on the man's head and hired some murderers to assassinate him. But of course every time there was an attempt on his life he could see it coming and disappeared. After many such attempts he asked himself if he had done some wrong in his past life. He understood that he had murdered his mother. So he resigned himself to accepting his fate and was finally killed.'

Phongyi explained that his past misdeed had been so heinous that no matter what good he did in this life he could not negate it.

So, I asked, is that how we should judge people – that he deserved to die despite being so good in later life?

'Judge the person by his actions now and in this life and do not condemn him for his wrongdoings in his previous life. His previous life only affects him and it is a matter for him.'

THINKING ABOUT THE PURPOSE OF LIFE

'Life is short; master the art of living rather than the fear of dying. You have lived only when you have lived for someone else. If you have lived only for yourself you leave nothing of value behind. What good has your life been?'

So the message is that we should make sacrifices for others, and that way we will be forgiven?

'The sacrifice and good work a person wishes to do should be with full desire and honest intent. It should come from the heart. The real reward is during your own lifetime for your good work.'

During my conversations with Phongyi I was beginning to realise that my own perspective on life, my philosophy, and even my beliefs were changing. The things that had been important to me were becoming less so, and as I let go of the world I had made for myself, I found myself becoming liberated. I felt freer than I had for a very long time – and in this I discovered that it was easier than I had imagined to open the door onto a pathway of spiritual growth. I wanted to know more – I just had to learn to let go.

'A jug fills

drop by drop'

Buddha

One afternoon Phongyi asked us to take a slightly longer lunch break so he could show us around the monastery grounds and take us to a local village.

One of his followers collected us in a four-wheel drive jeep. During our inspection of the monastery land we were politely probed for ideas which might make more of the natural assets. With my business experience, could I see a way of achieving an income from the land to help pay for the upkeep of the school and orphanage? The particular area Phongyi wanted to show us contained a natural hot spring. The overgrown land around it was mainly used as a thoroughfare for cattle.

After dinner, we sat down as usual to talk, but this time I was acutely aware it was my turn to perform.

I explained how we needed to find a way to make the school and orphanage as financially self-sufficient as possible rather than having to rely on donations that were precarious at the best of times. This meant starting some form of profitable business venture, and ideally one that would also provide employment for some of the children when they finished school. There were several possibilities.

Phongyi's widespread reputation as a wise and compassionate spiritual leader, and indeed the whole focus on the 'pure' image of the monastery Phaya Taung, was the key to this proposed enterprise. The community revered him, and so anything he endorsed was likely to sell as long as a consistently high standard was maintained.

I realised that the monks didn't have the time or experience to organise a business that, above all, would have to be run along highly ethical Buddhist principles based on benefiting the community. There were many boxes we needed to tick.

Taking all that into consideration I drew up a list of possibilities:

- Making use of the natural hot spring nearby and developing a spa.
- Opening the monastery as a spiritual retreat offering meditation and yoga.
- Using the buildings as a natural cold storage facility for the farmers' fresh produce.
- Developing a range of herbal products using the "Pure Essence" of Phaya Taung cachet.
- Using the natural cold spring behind the monastery to produce bottled mineral water.

After a great deal of debate we settled on a clear front-runner: natural bottled water. Not only would this provide great health benefits for the community by reducing illnesses from water-borne diseases; it was also wholly compliant with Buddhist principles. In Buddhism water symbolises purity, clarity and calmness, and reminds us to cleanse our minds and attain the state of *shamatha* or calm abiding.

Commercially, too, there were big advantages in that if we could establish and resource it properly, it would be scaleable. The monastery would be able to sell the mineral water and generate income to feed the children and provide for more facilities for the children. This would be a wonderful achievement. The conversation turned to naming the product. I initially suggested we used a picture of Phongyi on the label but he had a better idea, using an image of a novice monk – a Ko Yin. I could picture this in my mind and when I got back to London we produced a design that did just that, based on a photo MuMu had taken of the Ko Yin monks at the monastery.

The more I thought about the possibility of setting up a commercial fresh water bottling plant at Phaya Taung the more I became convinced that this wasn't just an impetuous notion but an entirely realistic one. If we were able to get the design and marketing of the bottled water right, emphasising the 'pure essence' of Phaya Taung and underscoring the careful and caring attention provided by Phongyi and the spiritual community there, we felt sure it could be successful. We would be able to raise enough money to feed the children every day. I was determined to put my plan in action.

My friends and family realised how passionate I was becoming about the project and wanted to help me. But I found it difficult to broach the subject of money with potential donors without appearing to sound too blunt or too forward.

I wrestled with this for some time, not knowing quite how to adopt the right approach. I needed their help but at the same time I was worried about intruding too much on people's time and good nature before I had a properly worked out plan. I trawled the internet trying to gather as much information as possible about water bottling machinery before narrowing it down to one or two possible suppliers. I found one in China who patiently answered all my naive questions allowing me to learn quite a lot about what the process involved. It seemed it wasn't as complicated as I had envisaged and the only real difficulty was the cost of setting up a sterile bottling unit. Next, I drew up a list of the challenges we had to overcome. I carefully listed everything except for one thing: how to find the necessary money.

First, we needed to test the source of the natural water. It was vital to establish that the water supply was clean and safe to use, and that would require a proper technical survey. Apart from anything else we also needed to know that the supply was both adequate and constant. We needed to be certain that the land was actually owned by the monastery, and that the monks possessed full legal entitlement to its resources. Planning permissions for extraction, and also rights of access for distribution by either boat or road, also had to be drawn up. Next came the machinery and equipment. We had to find the right type of filtering and bottling plant and somehow get it there and make it work. Then there was the question of distribution and sales. We were going to have to find someone who knew about that too. But, more than anything, we were going to need a lot of luck. And to our great surprise, our first lucky break came right out of the blue when MuMu and I were back home.

Some friends in London, Asif and Shakiba Rangoonwala, had asked MuMu if she could get them some traditional Burmese ear buds. These are quite unlike the cotton ones available at home. They are fearsomely long thin wooden sticks, a bit like chopsticks, curved at one end to scratch the inside of the ear and with a bird's feather at the other end. Quite why Asif wanted some of these strange instruments is anyone's guess but it was probably something to do with his late great philanthropic father who was born in Rangoon (Yangon).

We searched everywhere for these antiquated objects. It wasn't easy because they had long been superseded by more hygienic, cheap and efficient versions made in China at a fraction of the price. The shopkeepers either looked baffled or simply laughed at us. Our quest became something of a comical challenge. We toured the city's many bazaars but still drew a blank. Eventually MuMu called another of her many cousins, Ngni Ngni, to scour the more rural, traditional markets in Taunggyi where he finally found a handful of these precious ticklers. Back in London the ear buds proved a more than worthwhile investment. Asif was tickled pink (literally!) so much so that when I told him about the water project he immediately offered to help.

He was horrified to learn about the plight of the orphans and the hand to mouth existence of the monastery. I explained what we were trying to achieve and he was instantly won over, offering to fund a part of our enterprise through his family charity – the Rangoonwala Foundation.

But first he needed a business plan that he could put to the Foundation's trustees. Nothing too detailed, a couple of pages would do, but he needed them in the next day or so. I emailed him our plan and he called me the same evening to confirm he would support the project at the next trustees' meeting. He also wanted some more information. This time he needed a feasibility and impact report on the costs of the project and some budgets and sales forecasts. He needed more background information on the running costs and funding for the monastery school too.

I politely told him that a feasibility study wasn't possible given the meagre resources and negligible level of available on-site professional advice. There weren't any figures or statistics because there simply wasn't any data. However I said I would do whatever I could to put together the information. I knew I was going to need a lot of help from our friends in Burma and it would almost certainly require another trip there including spending some time at the monastery.

It was now June 2013 and, looking at my office commitments, the earliest I could go was October. I began to make the arrangements and collate as much information as possible before leaving. The first call was to Major to see if he would be around to accompany me and also find out if he could source the bottling machinery in Yangon or Taunggyi which would be a whole lot simpler than having to import it from China. In London my colleague, Rory St Johnston, had already completed the first draft of the bottle design and wrapper based on MuMu's photograph of the novice monks. Meanwhile we set about trying to commission some research into the quality of the existing water supply, and the potential benefits of providing clean drinking water for everyone at Phaya Taung. Major and Ting were lined up to help on the ground. With Phongyi praying for us, what could possibly go wrong?

But first, I had some unfinished business. I had written a short paper on my experience at the monastery, including the impact the computer teaching had had on the children, which I sent to a few close friends. Before even asking them for a contribution, I received a number of financial pledges. It meant I was able to order a dozen additional computers from the shop in Taunggyi. I didn't want to stretch my friends too much at this stage because I knew I was going to need their help for the much bigger and more costly water purification plant and bottling factory. With the extra computers we had the makings of a well-respected high tech facility along with some expert in-house tutors among the students.

At the end of July I received encouraging news. The monastery now had a sustainable power source. A benefactor, a Burmese American who had been introduced by Major, had installed a turbine at a nearby waterfall, with the power being fed via overhead cables across the rice fields to the monastery. The electricity supply had been tested and was reckoned to be stable enough to power the bottling plant. This was a terrific breakthrough and meant we had overcome one of the biggest obstacles to the project. Our luck was holding.

Now detailed planning work could begin in earnest. MuMu was unable to join me on this trip as she needed to spend some time with her ailing mother in Karachi. But Major confirmed he would meet me in Yangon at the end of September and be on hand to attend meetings with contractors and suppliers of such things as plastic bottles and labels. I needed to get my head around the manufacturing process and to pull together the financial data needed for the feasibility study. The plan was to collect the computers from Taunggyi before embarking on the seven-hour car and boat journey to set them up at the monastery. That, I hoped, would be the end of my involvement in the computers and I could then move on with getting the bottling plant up and running.

Apart from this latest trip to Burma, the rest of the year was already taken up with work and business trips. There was so much still to be done. Things were running ahead of me and I was still wrestling with the responsibilities of home, my firm and the challenge I had set myself to help the children. I was now seriously considering giving up my London career to free up enough time to finish what I had set out to do.

'Every man must decide whether he will walk in the light

of creative altruism or in the darkness of destructive selfishness.'

Martin Luther King

As the plane touched down in Yangon I couldn't help but smile. My first visit four years ago had been the beginning of a long journey. Along the way I had met many new friends and discovered a new meaning to my life. I had to finish this project.

However, this was all new to me, and the work was complicated. In order to keep my mind clearly fixed on the objectives in front of us, I was using meditation to visualise the water source on the hilltop behind Phaya Taung, the beautiful clear water flowing to the bottling plant at the monastery below and the children of the monastery healthy, happy and smiling. I knew that there were real benefits for the community, and my firm belief in this helped us confront the many hurdles we faced. In Mahayana Buddhism, the most important thing is motivation. If this is good and pure, everything will be workable. I felt totally supported by the knowledge that everyone involved shared this pure vision.

I spent the next three days in the city talking to companies and contacts that had expressed an interest in supplying the various bits of equipment we needed for the bottling plant. We had decided to identify and order all the equipment we would need at the same time as the testing of the water was being done. We would go ahead and build the plant anyway, and deal with the filtering issues later, once we had the results from the analysis. With the distances involved, time wasn't on our side.

It wasn't easy for several reasons. To begin with I could see all these people wondering who exactly they were dealing with. After all, here was a foreigner with a grandiose plan, trying to build something he knew nothing about. Not only that, but he wanted to build it in a remote part of the country. Despite this they were genuinely helpful. I think the tipping point was that this was a charity mission involving a Muslim wanting to support a Buddhist monastery.

In the end there was only one company big enough to take it on. A director of the company, Kyi Kyi Mar, became an enthusiastic supporter and promised to provide a detailed breakdown of the water filtering and bottling equipment that we would need. In the meantime we said we would deliver water samples for analysis and testing.

Our next mission was to buy the additional dozen or so computers in Taunggyi and deliver them to the monastery at Phaya Taung. We flew once again to Heho where Ting collected us and drove us to Taunggyi. Once we had picked up the computers we adjourned to the hotel at Nampan for the night, before setting off the following morning by canoe to the monastery some four hours away. This was the beginning of October and therefore the end of the monsoon season. The water level in the lake was really high and the conditions were perfect. We sped along under a clear blue sky, completely failing to take any precautions against getting sunburned. Our first glimpse of the monastery was of a crowd of children eagerly lined up to greet us – Major had phoned ahead to let them know when we would be arriving.

First we set up the computers. The children were so excited that it was difficult keeping them from interrupting while we connected up the necessary power supply to the classroom. To avoid a free-for-all we decided to organise a Computer Club. There were two goals. One was to use the computers to help teach them English. The other was to find the right person to take charge and run the computer classes. But before that, I was going to have to teach the teacher how to use the necessary software. Having done that, we needed to find someone else to organise and run the classes. I remembered one of the very first students we'd met at the monastery. May Than Nu was one of the older students, and an impressively quick learner, who was already teaching some of the younger children. Could she be the person we were looking for? The next day we got together with Phongyi, his deputy Oo Pazin, who was in overall charge of education, the teacher in charge of English, and May Than Nu. Everyone agreed May Than Nu was the right choice. She immediately set about organising a formal structure based on a Computer Club. There was simply no possibility that the relatively few computers available would be sufficient for everyone to be taught directly. We needed to build up teaching skills and then rotate the students at different levels of ability. By now there were

600 children in the monastery, and twelve computers. Eventually a hundred students were chosen for the first intake, and the plan was that successive waves of around a hundred students each would start to learn once each intake had attained a certain level.

Having started the classes and made sure the teachers and pupils knew what the structure of the day was to be, we turned our attention to the water bottling plant. The water source itself was about two miles from the monastery, but the access road was a tortuous mud track, which even our four-by-four struggled to negotiate. In the end it gave up altogether and we all piled into a truck to get there.

We collected the water samples we needed from various parts of the spring, and prepared to deliver them to our analyst back in Yangon. To be analysed properly, the samples had to be at the laboratory within 24 hours. This was easier said than done given the distance and logistics involved. It included the four-hour canoe trip followed by a seven-hour overnight coach journey, because there was no suitable flight. We crossed our fingers and sent the samples off with one of the students so that we could continue our work in getting the plans for the plant properly configured.

MuMu's cousin Ting had agreed to supervise the design and construction of the project, which included the site survey and assessing the best way of piping the water to the plant we were going to build. Ting came up with a design and system for piping the water to our proposed plant.

I was very conscious that time was short, and I had to complete the financial plan for Asif and other prospective backers in London. No one could be expected to commit funds before being sure we had the basis of a viable business. This involved finding out if there was even a demand for bottled water from the monastery. We knew we were not alone in wanting to supply water and there were already established companies out there. But would the 'pure essence' of

Phaya Taung water, endorsed by Phongyi's widespread reputation for goodness and probity, truly give us a positive advantage? We felt sure it would, but could we break into the market? There was only one way of finding out and that was to ask.

We were looking at supplying shops and villages in a 25-mile radius. We reckoned there were around five hundred hotels, shops and restaurants selling bottled water in the area around Inle at the time. But given the boom in tourism and the increasing number of new hotels springing up as a result of all the new development, this was likely to be a conservative estimate. We hoped to persuade them not just to buy our water, but to be willing to pay a premium for it. That would be a huge help in raising the money needed to feed and educate the growing number of children at the monastery. We had come up with the slogan 'one bottle feeds one child one meal'. The question was – would it work?

At the time around five million bottles of water were being sold to these outlets at the wholesale price of between 15 and 25 US$ cents depending on the size. We calculated we would need to capture at least ten per cent of the market. That worked out to half-a-million bottles a year if we were going to make enough money to fund the gap in the running costs of the school and orphanage at the monastery. It took a long time to gather in all the research but, having tested the numbers, we felt there was enough goodwill and sufficient commitment to make the project viable. With so many new hotels in the pipeline, we were convinced the position could only improve. Now we just needed to raise the $100k needed to build the plant!

Back in Yangon we were anxious to find out the results of the analysis tests on the water we had sent to the laboratory. We had sent three samples from different locations around the monastery. One was from the open water source, one from the bore well and the third from the mountain stream. We discovered that none of the samples was pure or for that matter even suitable for drinking without treatment.

All the samples were contaminated with natural bacteria to a greater or lesser extent. Although this was to be expected, it was hardly encouraging for all the people currently drinking it – and that included the children at the monastery. We needed to work quickly to find the right way to purify the water without losing its high levels of nutrients. Although we were initially disappointed, in a sense the analysis made us even more determined to make the project work. We simply had to ensure the monastery and the community nearby had a reliable supply of drinking water. I don't believe it's an exaggeration to say that it would be a life-saver for them.

Clean and safe water is something we all take for granted, but Burma still has a very long way to go on this issue. The children can hardly expect to live long and healthy lives unless this basic human need is provided. There is a general lack of understanding about sanitation and standards of hygiene remain low. Most homes in and around Inle Lake still rely on the lake for their drinking water and latrine disposal. The result is that the water is no longer fit to drink. There is a big effort to educate people and build new drains and toilets, but cholera and diarrhea are all too prevalent.

The design and infrastructure for the plant was there. The demand for the water was all too evident, and the technical know-how was available to make it happen. Much had been achieved, but none of it was going to be worth the paper it was written on unless we could raise the necessary funds to build this dream. I needed to head home and get working.

Once back in London I set about fundraising with a vengeance – contacting friends and clients to begin with, and then setting up a charity, The Inle Trust. Its core objectives were simple enough:

- Relieve the poverty of the people of Phaya Taung and

elsewhere in Burma and other developing countries.

- Provide – or assist in providing – clean water and sanitation.
- Support existing schools, and develop education and training schemes for the benefit of the children.

With money I had personally contributed and some cash from the Hollick Family Trust, the Freeman Family and the Eva Reckitt Trust, there was now $15k in the charity's bank account. Not bad for a few week's work. I was a man on a mission.

My friend Patrick Paul and his partner Nina were on holiday in Thailand and, since they were in that region and were keen to be involved, at their request I arranged for Major to take them to meet Phongyi in Phaya Taung. I knew that as soon as Patrick met Phongyi and saw what was happening at the monastery, he would be converted. So one weekend, as I was writing fundraising emails – and feeling somewhat despondent – Patrick contacted me and said that he would be happy to partner me on this project and match any funds that I was able to raise for The Inle Trust (www.inletrust. org.uk). To start with, he would send me a cheque for $15k (£10k) to match what I'd already accumulated. Within half an hour of this news, I'd booked flights for myself and MuMu to Burma as we now had sufficient funds to start the building work.

There was even better news to come. The following week, Meheen from the Rangoonwala Foundation confirmed that their family charity had approved a $40k grant. Asif had come through! Plans for a fundraising concert was also taking shape nicely, and in the following week I received several other personal donations. The money was flowing in and soon my thoughts turned from fundraising towards the work involved on the real mission – building the water filtering and bottling plant. As MuMu and I boarded the plane for Myanmar on February 26, 2014 I realised that I had two exceptional technical challenges to overcome:

1. The current advice from the machinery suppliers and the local consultant was to purify the water with a reverse osmosis (RO) process. It would strip out all hardness and nutrients, but the processed water would consequently be devoid of any taste. We needed to find a process that kept an acceptable level of natural flavour and minerals for good health while properly purifying the water.

2. The second challenge was to work out exactly how we could extract the mountain spring water from its underground source and pipe it to the factory site. Patrick, using his engineering skills, had made some drawings on how it might happen. But I had to translate them and team up with Ting, our architect, and the local engineer to come up with a proper plan.

My original proposal was to use the mountain spring to source good quality drinking water, with healthy amounts of nutrients and minerals. This would be made available to the children and villagers and the surplus sold to the local public. But the mountain spring was two miles away from the site and there were many hurdles to clear. It was tempting to go for the easier option of drilling a bore well next to the factory itself, but we decided against that because it was close to the lake and there was a strong chance that it could be contaminated. Patrick urged us to stay true to my original objective of providing the very best quality water.

The only real failure in life is not to be true to the best one knows.

Buddha

Following his own visit to the monastery, he set out the rough technical drawings of how we could extract the mountain water from the spring and pump it to a top holding tank high up on the hill. We planned to use gravity to flow the water from there to another holding tank by the filtering plant. In the end we compromised by building the top tank quite near to the spring itself, and pumping the water from there to the holding tank.

However, we were soon confronted by yet another obstacle. Even when purified, the mountain spring water, whilst containing a good supply of nutrients, proved to be very hard. There was an unacceptably high level of calcium for a premium mineral water, and we needed to remedy this. Most of the bottled water sold in Burma uses Reverse Osmosis for the simple reason that this process makes the water very clear and increases its shelf-life. As a result the available water purifying technology was based on this market demand. However this did not achieve our objective of providing the highest quality water. We wanted to retain all the natural goodness. We went through a number of complicated meetings with several water engineers in Yangon, but all of them were adamant that there was no other feasible method, I emailed Patrick in despair and said that perhaps it was better to 'go with the flow' and accept the easier RO solution. This meant compromising on the water quality. I reasoned somewhat unenthusiastically that it was likely to sell better because of the water clarity and longer shelf-life, and therefore would provide more funds to buy the children food.

The next day, I turned to my last resort – Kyi Kyi Mar, director of our machinery suppliers. I begged her to draw upon her experience and come up with a process that would achieve our objective. I assured her that we were prepared to take the business risk. After discussions with her own engineers, she came up with a process that introduced a more extensive UV and filtration system which achieved much of our objective whilst retaining the integrity of our product. This was an exciting breakthrough – we could after all have our pure Phaya Taung water, eliminating the hardness and retaining the goodness from all the minerals and nutrients. So far so good in theory, but we still didn't know how the UV filters would work in practice, and in addition we had no idea how it would taste.

Since our last visit to see Kyi Kyi Mar in October 2013, she had been curious as to why we had become involved with the monastery, raised the funds and set up the plans for the water plant. We were foreigners from a distant country, and Muslim too, yet we were working to help the Buddhist monk Phongyi and the orphaned children of the wars at Phaya Taung. So she had made a private trip to the monastery during her Christmas holidays. As a result she became committed to the project at a personal level.

Three days later MuMu and I were in Yangon, we had decided on the processing system to adopt, chosen the style of the bottle and the suppliers and commissioned the artwork for the wrapper. It was time to put all this into action and begin the project. We packed for our flight to Inle Lake. The plan was to meet up with Ting and Major at the hotel on the lake and spend the night there before heading for Phaya Taung monastery very early the next morning.

CHAPTER 11

CHANGING

'Everything that has a beginning has an ending.

Make peace with that and all will be well.'

Buddha

March 3, 2014 was a momentous day. Phongyi and 20 or so children were waiting for us at the pier. He had made sure most of the children we knew would be there, which made it an even more heart-warming welcome. Events moved at lightning speed from the moment we set foot on land.

On the way to Inle Lake we had decided that one way or another the water purification and bottling plant would be built, whichever source or filtering system were used. As we arrived, we saw that preparations on the factory site had already started. We informed Phongyi we were ready to begin work right away and asked if we could visit the mountain water source. Within minutes, some of Phongyi's ex-students arrived with motorcycles. Ting, the engineer, the mason, Oo Pazin and I headed off on an immensely bumpy three-mile ride.

After consultations with the engineer and mason, Ting drew up the instructions on how he wanted them to drill down towards the water source, pump the water to a water tank situated at the highest point on the hillside, from where it would be piped down to the purification and bottling plant. We returned to the building site and, to our amazement, found that the building measurements had been marked out and some excavation work already started. Much of the plinth on which the building was to stand was already in place. A hundred or so students had volunteered and helped.

Phongyi also announced that it was an auspicious day to bless the start of the building. All the students from the monastery gathered around and Phongyi asked the four of us – Major, Ting, Bo Kyaw and me – each to hammer a wooden stake at one corner of the building. MuMu was asked to pour clean scented water on these foundations and Phongyi prayed for the success of the venture.

By the time we returned for our next visit we had come a long way, but there was much more to do. Nothing is ever straightforward in Burma, as the country gradually emerges from its past into the modern world. The industrial and commercial infrastructure is inconsistent and often frustrating, and trying to get anything done that requires permissions and investment is unpredictable. Arriving in the middle of the monsoon season didn't help. At this time of year the lush green countryside quickly turns brown and everything not already bogged down in paperwork becomes clogged in mud. Transport is difficult at the best of times but during the monsoon it can become impossible.

But having come this far we knew we would do everything we could to achieve our goals. The words of Buddha – always so wise – came to mind.

'Do not dwell in the past; do not dream of the future,
concentrate the mind on the present moment.'

Buddha

Four years had passed since I first set eyes on the monastery at Phaya Taung. We had made a good start with the computers and teaching, and we had planned the water purification plant. Now we had to make it a reality. We had our dreams of what could be achieved for the community, but to date we hadn't set eyes on a drop of clear water. Well, not from the ground anyway.

In Yangon there were hurdles to overcome. The second cash instalment to Kyi Kyi Mar was delayed, but I knew from past experience that things have a way of working out, and sure enough the money turned up. As a favour she threw in a supply of bottles and other ancillary equipment, including an ingenious piece of equipment to seal the bottle tops. The bottling machinery would be dispatched from Yangon by truck, taking a couple of days to reach the lakeside at Nyaung Shwe, ready for the onward trip by boat.

We met with the people supplying the bottle tops and those printing the bottle wrappers. I left enough money with our new PNO friend Khun Maung Saung to pay for everything and arrange to have it delivered over the next two weeks. As we talked to our friends, we became aware of the uneasy tension between the Buddhists and Muslims in parts of the country, which threatened to destabilise the all-important tourist industry. Quietly I hoped that the story of a Muslim helping a Buddhist monk might serve as an inspiration to others.

Time was going to be tight. On arriving at the airport for Inle at HeHo, we were met by Major who took us straight to the pier and our boat for the journey to the monastery. A sense of calm befell me. I felt I was back where I belonged. The hustle and bustle of Yangon, and the trials of organising the funds and machinery for the plant felt a long way off. Right now I was happy to be back within reach of the monastery and the children.

The sky was overcast and cloudy and we could see localised bursts of rain spreading from patches of dark clouds in the sky. This was a sure sign that we were witnessing the beginnings of the monsoon season. Luckily, despite the occasional short shower, we mostly kept dry. Major quickly drifted off to sleep. I imagined he was used to snatching sleep wherever and whenever he could during his cattle smuggling days. When we reached the hotel at Inle, we were welcomed in the usual way, but this time by a somewhat improvised kitchen band. I spotted cousin Ting and Bo Kyaw both beaming away on the jetty.

Over dinner we turned to the main purpose of our trip – the water project. In my mind I drew up a list of the priorities. I had to check on the progress of the machinery due by road and the difficult five-hour boat journey to the monastery; develop the design and production of the wrapper and bottle tops; keep a careful eye on the money situation; meet with the engineer and with Ting, our guiding hand on the project, to discuss the water flow and judge the optimum size for the water storage tanks.

All the whisky, green tea and excitement made sleep impossible that night, and so I lay awake going over and over the details. Thankfully the next day was a rest day so we went out in the boat shopping. We left for the monastery very early the following morning because Ting had to be back that evening and so I wanted to make the most of his time.

As we approached the jetty we could see a very enthusiastic welcoming party of at least a hundred students lined up to greet us. Our spirits were hugely lifted – their happy smiles and warm greetings were infectious. We walked up the hill and I could hardly believe what I saw.

An immaculate new building had appeared, painted brightly in yellow and green. Looking through the open doorway, I noticed the sparkling tiled floor. This was the new Ko Yin Mineral Water factory, finished. I was amazed. Phongyi had made sure it would be a surprise. He was always one step ahead, and had delivered far beyond my expectations. This was the best possible present I could have received, but I knew we had a long way to go before we would start seeing Ko Yin water bottles rolling off the production line. There would be some uncomfortable bumps and tight turns to negotiate along the way.

After lunch, Ting and I went through the accounts with Phongyi's assistant and prepared an estimate of future funding requirements. One unexpected item was the cost of the two concrete water tanks, now with an enlarged capacity of 200,000 gallons. Thankfully the fundraising show we put on in London had raised £13k, and so we had enough cash in hand to pay for them.

Our son Nadir wanted to try some sort of activity with the children. The teachers suggested a class in English reading and that perhaps he could perform a few English songs for them on his guitar.

Word got around that a young visitor to the monastery was playing songs on the guitar and soon an avalanche of students swept into the open assembly hall. I reckoned there must have been over 500 in the audience. Phongyi produced his preaching microphone and the concert began. Nadir performed six or seven songs to rapturous applause. Major then invited the other children to join in and perform, offering a reward of 5000 kyats (five US dollars).

Several did, and it turned into a talent show. It was a completely impromptu and really enjoyable moment with our new Phaya Taung family.

After the concert, Phongyi talked to the children and explained how people so far away cared for them and contributed towards their well-being and welfare. They were compassionate and kind-hearted and wanted them to have a better life, even though they had never even met or seen them.

That evening, soon after dinner was served, Phongyi arrived and answered more of my questions on the meaning of life. He was patient and wise. On an earlier visit, I had asked him about finding happiness, and he had replied:

'Happiness comes to your heart through your ways. Change the way you behave and improve as a human being.'

I wanted to learn more. I asked how do you improve as a human being?

'Follow nature's law; develop spiritually with every advancing age of your life, accept the changes and strive to improve as a human being at every stage.

You can improve at every stage of your life: the development is a gradual process of spiritual transformation. As a young person, you can be kind and considerate and helpful to your friends and family.

As you get older and go to work, you can assist your colleagues when they need a helping hand or help with voluntary work in your spare time; when you get married and have children, bring them up with love and kindness. Be a good role model and they will learn from your ways.

And finally when you are much older, you will be ready and well placed to be able to make a more profound contribution to the welfare of your fellow human beings.

When worldly knowledge is harnessed with good intent for moral
ends, it can bring maximum benefit and incredible happiness.'

I said, not everyone develops in the same way and at the same pace.
Why are some young people sensitive and caring even as children
whilst others, even when they are old, remain ignorant?

'In Buddhist philosophy, all of us bring our consciousness from our
past lives. Depending upon our deeds in previous lives, we come back
as a more enlightened human being if we have been a good person or
as a regressed being if we have been a bad person.'

He explained how you can also change your fortunes in this life
by your good deeds.

'If one is more enlightened from a previous life, it is often possible
to follow the spiritual path even earlier in this life.'

Phongyi told me that another way of putting it is that when you are
reborn, depending upon your deeds in your previous lives, you are
reborn as an angel or as an unfortunate; or as an animal; or a person
who suffers in hell.

Turning to the subject of prayer and meditation, I asked why
he spent virtually all his time helping the children while the other
monks spent more praying?

'Both methods are credible: either you can do good deeds directly as
I am fortunate enough to be able to do. Other monks who practice
and teach prayer impart their wisdom to others and facilitate them
to become better persons. I would also like to add that the practice
of meditation is often misunderstood in the West. It is not just the
practice of relaxation of the mind but it has a much more profound
purpose: that of becoming a peaceful person who fully understands
the laws of nature and is able to act with utmost compassion with his
fellow human beings. Whilst the attainment of such compassion is

enlightening it also brings with it a duty of purpose and action.'

So far I had avoided asking Phongyi anything that might be seen as political, but given that the racial violence between Buddhists and Muslims in Rakhine State was becoming extreme I wanted to hear what a Buddhist monk had to say about this complete breakdown of honesty and tolerance between the faiths. Buddhism, I said, is such a peaceful practice – how is it that some Buddhist monks justify aggression and preach violence?

Such monks rise up to defend their faith. But they should act with utmost compassion, forgiveness and tolerance. The only solution is education and, in particular, the understanding of each others points of view by the monks and everyone of both religions – and always, of course, the practice of compassion. From a Buddhist perspective, I would urge people to study the concept of cause and effect, or karma.

Buddhism teaches that the law of cause and effect underlies the workings of all phenomena. Positive thoughts, words and actions create positive effects in our lives, leading to happiness. Negative thoughts, words and actions on the other hand – those that in some way undermine the dignity of life – lead to unhappiness. This is the general concept of karma.

Furthermore, we must remind ourselves that we own nothing in this world, not even our own body. We can leave nothing behind (but we can take with us the merits of our good deeds) other than the effect of our good deeds.

Lead by example to show compassion towards all our fellow human beings. Humanity both supersedes and is yet intrinsic in most religious belief and practice. A good example is here at the monastery we accept children of all races and religions and they are allowed to practice their faith. Another good example is you, Feroze. You are a Muslim helping a Buddhist monastery. Further, think of the number of English people – Christians, Hindus, Muslims, Jews and so on –

who have all come together to contribute and help in this Buddhist monastery project.

I continued in the same vein and asked Phongyi for his comment on the Rakhine. "What are your comments on the Rakhine issue whereby some 500,000 Rohingyas have been forced to flee from their home in Myanmar across the border to take refuge in Bangladesh? In particular the reports of torture and killing of these desperate people?"

Killing and torture of human beings is totally unacceptable. If a person pinched himself – let alone suffered torture – he would feel the pain and realise the other person's suffering. Every human being is equal and all of us have to be tolerant and forgiving.

"What we are witnessing is extreme racial violence between Muslims and Buddhists. This conflict and the vast majority of other conflicts in the world have a religious dimension with each religion claiming supremacy over the other. What began as a message of love has now become completely hollow and distorted. Should we just eliminate religion as perhaps this would result in a more peaceful world?"

It is important to note that in Buddhism ....Buddha emphasised to people not to follow him blindly. But to decide for yourself what is right or wrong.

"All religions proclaim the spiritual path, and yet and have different ways of exploring it. For example Sufism or zikr in Islam, the Trinity and the power of prayer in Christianity, Vipassana, or seeing things as they really are, in Buddhism. What is your view on finding a deeper sense of spirituality which at its heart is surely a form of meditation?"

Meditation (Vipassana) is the Buddha way. With meditation you will be peaceful inside. If you are peaceful inside you will be peaceful on the outside ......peaceful in the way you feel and behave with others.

As the evening drew to a close I noticed for the first time that Phongyi looked tired and even stressed. When I asked why, he explained that another two hundred children had recently arrived, and needed taking care of. This brought the total number of children in the monastery to around 800.

'I cannot refuse them but all the facilities here are stretched well beyond capacity. I even got angry with someone today and I feel that I have sinned in so doing.'

'You will not be punished for your anger,

you will be punished by your anger.'

Buddha

CHAPTER 12

REWARDING

'Be kind whenever possible. It is always possible.'

His Holiness the Dalai Lama

It was then that I realised that my work was far from finished, not just in putting up these facilities, but more importantly in helping to create a sustainable management structure so that the whole burden did not rest solely on Phongyi's shoulders.

We all had concerns, not just about providing enough food and shelter, but about the lack of adequate sanitation. There were very few toilets and so unsurprisingly the children were using the forest and lake. As a result disease was prevalent and, with the nearest doctor several miles away by boat and the numbers of children rising continually, the situation was becoming urgent. The other monks were going to have to help.

Of course, there would be dangers to introducing a formal management culture. It could erode the charm of the place and alter the traditional way the monastery had been run for the last quarter of a century. But I didn't think the place could easily survive without changing. We needed to fuse Buddhist spiritual wisdom with modern business practice.

The monsoon had now taken hold in earnest. We were getting ready to turn in when at around midnight, in the middle of a torrential downpour, a student came running in to announce that the boat had arrived loaded with machinery. We ran to the pier to find an army of students starting to unload the cargo. It was dark, and mud made the ground slippery. The boatman suggested that the heavier machinery should wait until morning when it would be light and hopefully drier. At around seven the next morning, the children called me to watch the unloading of the rest of the cargo.

Soon we had the building completed, the machinery under cover, and a stock of empty bottles – but as yet, no spring water. There was a well to dig and pipes to lay to carry the water the two miles to the bottling plant. The reinforced concrete tanks still had to be built, and in the new building there was still the internal partitioning, plumbing and electrics to complete. All this would have to wait until the next time Ting was on site with the specialist materials and builders from Taunggyi.

Meanwhile, there had been another unsuccessful attempt to sink a concrete barrel deep enough to create a useable well. As there was nothing further we could do on the building site for the moment, I suggested we looked at training up the first few employees and volunteers who would be working in the bottling plant. Bo Kyaw offered to arrange for them to work as interns at the PNO-owned water factory in Taunggyi. Ironically, this would be one of our main competitors. Accordingly, we drew up a timetable of about a month to complete the construction works, allowing a testing period of another month for the filtration system. I planned to return in the middle of August to launch the product in readiness for the pagoda festival in September and the beginning of the tourist season.

We still had a tremendous amount to do before the plant was up and running, and the team was apprehensive about the scale of the engineering work required to complete the holding tanks and the pipework, and the challenge of getting to grips with the science of water purification.

The day we started back for London I had mixed emotions on leaving Inle Lake. I realised that with the work on the water purification and bottling plant well underway, the project was coming to some sort of conclusion. But the idea of simply walking away from the children and their future didn't bear thinking about. I was already contemplating the next phase.

Meanwhile, in order to maximise the potential of the work so far completed, and to raise awareness of the project, I had decided to write a book. Having found a publisher at home, I was hoping to do the same in Burma and Pakistan. The wider message and especially the prospect of spreading the word in the Asian sub-continent would be enormously helpful, but how to set about doing this?

During one of my meetings with a long-standing client Khalid Awan, chairman of a major logistics group based in the UAE and Pakistan, he asked if I would consider joining the board as a non-executive director. It would involve quarterly meetings in Dubai or Pakistan and he would ensure that my travel arrangements would be comfortable. There was also an attractive fee involved. It also meant I could spend some quality time with my parents in Karachi. I accepted without hesitation.

Two weeks before I was due to attend my first board meeting, Khalid called me in London to say the meeting was postponed, but since the travel arrangements had already been made it would be great if I could still come – we could have some informal discussions together. But it was what he also added during the conversation that really caught my attention. The group owned an online bookseller and was planning a series of events with authors who had written true stories that were inspirational and life-changing. Khalid suggested they launch with my own book. Here was the opportunity I desperately needed to promote my message to a completely new audience. Khalid suggested a few names of well-known journalists he could ask to interview me, and he also proposed doing it himself. He assured me that my audience would include the crème de la crème of Pakistan society. His wife Saadia would pull in her extensive contacts to ensure the right people were there. It was going to be the perfect opportunity to sell books and to do some fundraising for The Inle Trust. Although this left only two weeks to organise the event, Khalid was convinced it could be done.

Khalid picked me up from the airport in Karachi. He had managed to book the book launch venue for the following week on my last full day in Karachi, and we drove straight there to finalise the programme. The venue was perfect - an arty bohemian library and art gallery cum social centre called The Second Floor, also known as T2F.

Sometimes even the best-laid plans can go awry. The very next day, the company's CEO had to stand down from the business, which meant that Khalid needed to step in. He hadn't carried out a hands-on role with the business for at least 15 years, and getting his feet back under the desk was a time-consuming challenge. To add to the strain, his wife Saadia had to fly to London because a close relative had been taken seriously ill. With only ten days to go, I was feeling apprehensive, but as it turned out something much bigger was about to happen.

During my earlier visits to the monastery, I had seen how much Phongyi struggled to house, feed and educate so many children.

I felt that he really needed some divine intervention. In my usual naïve way, disregarding all protocol, I suggested asking His Holiness the Dalai Lama to help. Phongyi said that he was a lowly monk and did not feel worthy to propose this, nor did he feel it was his place to make His Holiness aware of the situation at this monastery. So I offered instead. I had no idea how to go about it, so I took a leaf out of His Holiness the Dalai Lama's own book.

'With realisation of one's own potential and self-confidence in one's ability one can build a better world.'

His Holiness the Dalai Lama

As soon as the book had been first published in May 2014, I sent a copy to His Holiness. I wasn't sure what to expect. Apart from drawing attention to the work we were doing, I suppose I was hoping for some sort of endorsement, assuming he ever received the book. I was aware that, since withdrawing from his political role in the Central Tibetan Administration in 2011, His Holiness rarely, if ever, endorsed books. Two days before the book launch in Karachi I received an email:

From: <xxxxxxxxxxx.com>
Date: 30 July 2014 08:43:59 BST
To: <feroze.dada@xxxxxxx.co.uk> Subject: endorsement
Dear Feroze,
The Office of His Holiness the Dalai Lama received your letter
and the book Children of the Revolution.
Our secretary has decided to present your request to His
Holiness. So, we will send you an endorsement/blessing for the
book by His Holiness as soon as it is ready.
Regards,

I had to read the email several times for it to register. It dawned
on me that such an endorsement could provide a wider international
dimension for the book and therefore help to generate some more
much-needed money for the charity. Much as the success of the
computer project at the monastery had led to the setting up of a
proper registered charity, and then given rise to the water project,
so His Holiness' interest in the topic of the book could now help to
increase its audience dramatically. This was a game changer for us.

Equally it placed an enormous responsibility on me to make
the very best use of this accolade for the charity and ensure that we
adhered to the highest standards. I was determined to make His
Holiness proud of his trust in me, and in the work we were doing.

After scrambling around and making much use of social media,
we managed to get the book launch on track. It was all very last
minute and involved arranging for a pile of books to be couriered for
the guests and panelists. In the end, the event was fully subscribed
and, judging from the feedback, it was very successful. Khalid proved
to be a calm and insightful interviewer and, because of our personal
chemistry, he was able to ensure that he got the best out of me. There

was one potentially awkward moment but I was prepared for it.

It came when a member of the audience asked why a Muslim was helping a Buddhist monk when his fellow monks were in conflict with Muslims. Since I had already debated this point with Phongyi, I was able to answer with confidence and genuine belief. I was relieved when many in the audience stood up to defend my humanitarian point of view.

I couldn't believe it, but afterwards there was a long queue of people asking me to sign copies of the book for which they had willingly paid the full UK retail price. The stock of books we had couriered from London was sold out.

I was happy but exhausted. All through the following day my mobile didn't stop ringing and social media sites went into overdrive. Those who had not turned up wanted to buy the book, magazines wanted interviews, and bookshops wanted copies. The launch hadn't made the inside book review pages but it was featured on the front page of the largest circulation English newspaper in Pakistan. 'Stories of Hope and Heroism' ran the headline, a reference to what we were doing in the face of so much turmoil in the country.

On the flight back to London, I pondered our next steps and tried to think how to make the most of His Holiness The Dalai Lama's endorsement if it came through. While I was on a mission to make the monastery itself self-sustaining, I also knew that I now had the opportunity to make The Inle Trust into a much more meaningful charity. But, like Phongyi, although I had my begging bowl I wanted to make sure we provided something wonderful in return. I was working on a number of different business ideas, including releasing a Pa'O folk song. I already had songwriter Charlie Freeman composing the English version and the renowned music guru Ric Salmon producing it. I had built up my London accounting practice 25 years ago, brick by brick. Now I would be starting all over again.

This time I needed to do it faster and smarter. So I hit the reset button and started to move my work away from my business responsibilities. In order to enable me to concentrate more on The Inle Trust, I agreed an exit plan with our CEO, and immediately felt liberated. I knew this was what I wanted to do more than anything, and I needed to be as effective as possible. In looking at the way my time had been spent I found I could have been better at planning for the things I wanted to accomplish. Each day is a link in the chain that makes up our lives, so on a practical level I wanted to live in the most balanced way I could and to make my actions as meaningful as possible. Facing a new situation with awareness is a crucial part of the best way to take responsibility. I was very mindful of this as I was changing emphasis and opening my heart to the children at Phaya Taung monastery.

CHAPTER 13

HEALING

'I never see what has been done.

I only see what remains to be done.'

Buddha

Burma has the highest infant mortality rate of all ASEAN member countries. According to UNICEF, around 56,000 children under the age of five die there every year from largely preventable diseases. Of these more than 40,000 are less than a month old. One of the main reasons behind this is the lack of safe drinking water.

The situation is improving, but pressures on the country's infrastructure make the government target of providing clean drinking water to everyone a major challenge. According to the UN, deforestation from logging, industrial development, new housing and agriculture – which currently uses 75% of water resources – all add to the challenge.

Globally there are nearly 800 million people without access to drinking water and three times as many without adequate sanitation. Every minute of every hour of every day, a child dies from water-related illnesses.

All this is a sobering thought, and I am acutely aware that what we have been attempting at Phaya Taung is only a drop in the ocean.

But I hope that where we lead others will follow. It has been an incredible experience: frustrating and bewildering certainly, and at times physically draining, but extraordinarily rewarding. We were getting back far more than we were giving as we stumbled and sprinted our way along the path we had set out on, which twisted and turned in unexpected ways all along the journey.

As soon as I returned to London from launching the book in Karachi I started planning my next trip to Burma. There was, as usual, much to do. We had lined up meetings in Yangon with prospective local publishers and various bookshops, and looked into the feasibility of printing a paperback edition. The original hardcover edition was selling strongly in the Myanmar Book Centre and in some of the other hotels by Inle Lake.

When we arrived back in Yangon there were problems. We urgently needed to resolve everything with the bottling equipment suppliers and bottle manufacturers. Whilst the bottle design was beautiful, because of its clean cylindrical shape, we were told it would require almost twice as much plastic to support the design than the other brands were using. Put simply, it was going to cost too much. However, after explaining the charitable purpose, the manufacturer had a change of heart. The managing director intervened and promised to find a solution and reduce the price. He would need time to think it through, and in the meantime he suggested we use one of the off-the-shelf designs we had already identified as being possible. After three days of meetings in Yangon, we left for Inle Lake.

My heart sank when we were picked up at the airport and Major told us that not much had happened in the two months since our last visit. In fact, he said that work on the plant had ground to a halt. I had a feeling worse was to come. It didn't take long for me to be proved right. Although the water filtration and bottling plant was complete, none of the services such as electricity or plumbing had been installed. And the full partitioning for the air conditioning still had to go in.

I was feeling apprehensive on arriving at the lake, having been told there had been a personality clash between the engineer and Ting, our architect. Communication between them had often been tense, and I could sense that something wasn't right as soon as we got to the hotel. Ting was already there but on this occasion he didn't rush to greet me and wouldn't look me in the eye. Now I knew we had a big problem on our hands. This was not the Ting I knew.

I arranged for a different engineer and made it clear that he would have to remain on site at the monastery until the job was finished, whatever Ting did. I decided, too, that I would stay until the installation was completed.

We had to get the show back on the road. Allocating blame wasn't the answer. Raising spirits and team morale was. A lot of people had given generously to the project and we all shared the responsibility to ensure the job was finished. All the goodwill and hard work so far would come to nothing unless the water started flowing.

Ting's view was that the engineer's job was just to fix the machinery – Ting was the project architect and should be left alone to get on with the design and construction, inside and out. He didn't take kindly to what he saw as interference from the engineer.

What he hadn't taken on board was that the whole thing had to be configured and finished in such a way as to comply with health and safety requirements in order to obtain the necessary certification to operate a commercial water factory. Airtight partitions were needed at different stages in the filtration process to ensure the highest level of hygiene. Kyi Kyi Mar and her team knew what to do: they had been responsible for many similar water projects. Ting had designed and built mainly domestic and office buildings, and he had no experience of setting up a water filtration plant to satisfy the regulations. However, having taken a stand, Ting felt he couldn't back down without losing face.

The whole purpose of the project, i.e. helping the children, was in danger of being lost in the midst of professional differences. I was reminded of Buddha's quote.

'Wear your ego like a loose-fitting garment'

Buddha

I had to find a way for us all to shed our egos and move forward. I was going to have to persuade Ting to meet face to face with the engineer and agree roles and responsibilities. I gave myself 24 hours to sort out their differences.

That night I couldn't sleep. I prayed that we could get the project back on track for the sake of the children, and that all of us could abandon ego and set aside our pride. I felt that I had taken my eye off the ball by spending so much time promoting my book and enjoying the personal limelight, rather than ensuring everything at the monastery was running smoothly and to time.

From my own business experience, I knew that while most well-planned projects run with their own momentum, there are almost always one or two sticking points – and more often than not they are to do with people management. Being able to navigate the correct path at critical points was crucial. The next few days at Phaya Taung could be make or break. I needed to draw on all my experience to move forward with wisdom and tact. As Buddha so wisely said:

'If you do not change direction,

you may end up where you are heading'

Buddha

The night before leaving for the monastery the team met for dinner. I reminded them – Major, Bo Kyaw, Ting, and my wife MuMu – that with the publication of the book and the press coverage we had received, many people from different parts of the world would be watching what happened. Even His Holiness the Dalai Lama had indicated that he would give it his blessing. We carried a huge burden of responsibility. I would not return from the monastery until the factory was in production.

We decided to travel in only one boat so that no one could leave by themselves. Ting and Bo Kyaw would be staying overnight in the relative comfort of a hotel twenty minutes away in Samkar, while MuMu, Major and I would sleep as normal at the monastery.

We called Phongyi who confirmed that the engineer had arrived. We asked him to make sure he held onto him until we arrived, and that his electrician and plumber were at hand and ready to work for as long as it took. In the meantime, Phongyi should order any necessary supplies right away so that nothing would delay the start.

Next morning we left early by boat and arrived at the monastery mid-morning. Where was the welcoming committee? This looked ominous. Instead of the usual throng of happy smiling faces, there was just a handful of students.

The engineer stood outside the factory door looking listless. I took him aside and looked him in the eyes.

'You aren't doing this work for me, for Ting or even Phongyi – it's for the children. So please do your very best.'

My words seemed to have the desired effect and soon the whole team was back at work. Everyone knew there was a great deal at stake. This was the last chance to finish what we had spent so much time, effort and money to plan and build. For the next 36 hours, we all worked feverishly. The engineer, plumber and electrician continued throughout much of the night, and a hundred or so of the older students, led by Phongyi, helped dig the courses and lay the remaining water pipes that would feed from the reservoirs into the plant.

By the following morning the filtration system had been tested, the pipes had been connected to the reservoirs, and the work on the airtight partitions was largely completed. I had never witnessed or taken part in such an intensive and motivated team effort.

EVERYTHING IS WORKABLE

What holds us back from living mindfully is clinging to our self, and to our self-importance. Our belief in me, or what is mine, distracts us from the path of the dhamma and we need to change our habits if we are to grow. There is no 'self' and no 'other' – we all want the same, which is to be happy.

We need to integrate meditation and mindfulness into everything that we do, and to train our minds towards achieving non-distraction.

'It is not as if we find the ego and then throw it out, it was never there in the first place. What we find is its absence.

The discovery of this absence is the experience of emptiness.'

His Holiness the Dalai Lama

A glimpse of egolessness can release great energy and creativity, and we discover that everything in our lives becomes workable.

THE NOBLE EIGHTFOLD PATH

SHILA – OR MORALITY

Right Speech

Right Action

Right Livelihood

SAMADHI – OR MEDITATION

Right Effort

Mindfulness

Concentration

PRAJNA – OR WISDOM

Right Understanding

Right Resolve

When we cling to ideas, to possessions, to our separateness from others, or to the way things are supposed to be, we suffer. The more we learn to let go and live with the ever-changing nature of this world, the more we can live in peace.

Living in the reality of the present – and coming back to this moment, to where we are, abandoning the conflict in our minds about our imagined futures or past regrets – leads us to respond to the world with compassion. The Eightfold Path teaches us to rediscover our own true nature and to live with a wise heart.

Even with all this going on, we still managed to snatch a few hours with Phongyi. Needless to say, I had more questions for him:

RAISING CHILDREN

Why do I see so many young people turning to drugs, alcohol or suffering from psychological illnesses, particularly children from families with parents who have been high achievers?
'Parents must do the best for their children, be good role models, and guide and educate them. But parents should never be unhappy or disappointed if their children do not live up to their expectations. Such a burden of expectation is often too difficult for a young person to carry. Each human being must have the freedom to travel their own path.'

'No one saves us but ourselves –

No one can and no one may.

We ourselves must walk the path.'

Buddha

HONESTY

Honesty is undoubtedly a great virtue. But it isn't always so easy to practice.

'Telling the truth is not always easy as it requires tact, so as not to be hurtful, and wisdom in the way you exercise it. In particular, if you are pointing out a wrong deed committed by someone or you are giving advice with honest intent for that person to change their ways, they may not like it at that time.

'Always be honest when you intend to do good by telling the truth. If you do not expect a good outcome from it, exercise such honesty sparingly and with great care as it can be hurtful for no good purpose.'

Is it justifiable to lie if you expect it would achieve a good outcome?

'A lie can never have a good outcome. It may well divert or delay the issue for the time being but will not resolve it.'

COMPASSION

Earlier, you said, in the context of our discussions on interfaith, 'Exercise compassion, forgiveness and tolerance.' What do these terms actually mean?

'Compassion is a human quality (of feeling the suffering of others) which we all have the potential to enact within us. However, to feel true compassion, you need to put yourself in the other person's position. Furthermore, you also need to think how you would like the other person to act towards you if you were in that predicament yourself.

'You will then naturally act in such a compassionate way so as to relieve the other person's pain and suffering.'

FORGIVENESS

'It is not necessary to exercise forgiveness for the benefit of those who have harmed you. They will pay the price for their own misdeeds. If you are unable to let go forgiveness is necessary for your own well-being.'

It is easy to say 'I forgive' but how do you feel the benefit of the forgiveness?

'Say to yourself that you seek no revenge. Have no fire in your heart. Rain your kindness equally on the just and unjust alike. A tree gives shade to all, including the woodcutter.'

TOLERANCE

'Life is short and there is much to do without the distraction of being upset by minor misdeeds and differences – difference in religion, race, culture and so on. We are all fallible as human beings.

'However, from a practical perspective, if you don't exercise tolerance, minor issues can become major upheavals. Exercise tolerance even if the other party does not reciprocate. In the fullness of time, they will more than likely learn to reciprocate with tolerance in the same way.'

LOVE

Here we are talking about love for family and friends, teachers and companions.

'To understand true love you have to learn to perfect this love in yourself. To be true to yourself you have to be respectful, honest and sincere. Hence you also need to improve yourself and your own habits first.

'Only when you have learnt these qualities yourself can you share them with others in a pure way. Otherwise the love you give will itself be tainted.'

Does everyone know how to share love?

'To give love to others you need to be compassionate and have the ability to empathise – to put yourself in the other person's place.'

Should we expect the love we give to others be reciprocated?

'No, we should not expect anything in return. Sometimes the recipient of our love is incapable of understanding what they are receiving. For example, some children will take love from a parent and take it for granted.'

SUICIDE AND EUTHANASIA

What about when you are shocked and saddened to hear that someone you had admired has taken their own life – a gifted individual who had given so much joy and who no doubt would have continued to do so?

'The Buddhist belief is that the time and the manner in which we will die is predestined. However, our good deeds in our lifetime can favourably change to some extent the predestined outcome. Taking a life when you cannot give a life, either your own or someone else's, is equally sinful.

'But from a practical perspective, an individual usually takes his own life because they are mentally unstable or are unhappy in this world.'

CREATION AND REINCARNATION

What is the sense of our place in creation in Buddhism?
'To find the answer you will need to look beyond the bones of our previous 13 reincarnations. Better to look forward - you will gain nothing by looking back. We alone are responsible for our path to end suffering and find enlightenment.'

What happens when we die?
'The essence of our consciousness continues. To grow again the papaya seed is sown and not the whole papaya. Most people come back to life, depending upon their deeds and actions during their lifetime as:

    1.   Angel
    2.   Human
    3.   Animal
    4.   Hell (a person in hell)
    5.   Demon

Who decides the status of our next reincarnation?
'Our own deeds – the quality of the papaya seed will depend on the quality of the papaya'.

When do we cease to come back to life in the human realm, and become spiritually awake and truly enlightened?
'When we cease to have greed or attachment to the material world, we cease to exist – like the candle whose flame has flickered out.'

Are we able to perceive or remember our previous lives?
'Very few do, either as experience in our everyday lives when we meet people we may have known, or, exceptionally, in dreams or when in meditation.'

How can we improve our reincarnation – other than by doing good deeds during our lifetime?
'By meditation – so that at the time of passing our consciousness is peaceful.'

THE FUTURE OF HUMANITY

When you look at the way in which the world is changing, are you optimistic or pessimistic about the future?
'I am concerned that the world is developing very fast and people are getting more and more materialistic. There is a continued expectation to increase our materialist standard of living. The gap between the rich and the poor is immense; in other words, human beings are become increasingly greedy. Even the capitalistic economic-democratic political system is failing.

'Conversely our quest for spiritual development continues to decline and people are getting increasingly dissatisfied with the manner in which religions are practiced and the human atrocities carried out in the name of religion.'

It's clear you don't see a rosy picture for humanity. What can you say to give us hope for the future?
'We need to control our greed by being less materialistic and at the

same time strive to develop spiritually. Be charitable with an open heart and good intent. That way you will feel happier and have a peaceful life. You will naturally begin to feel compassionate and caring and help your fellow human beings.

'*Many of these changes will manifest themselves fully if they are instilled in people when they are young, in the next generation.*'

How do you propose that we get this message across?

'*The problem we have is that we practice religion in a way that makes us captive to the rituals and forget the underlying principles which are common in all major religions. What we need is a simple and universal code of conduct that the whole world – countries, organisations and individuals – willingly sign up to and aspire to uphold.*'

Phongyi returned to his theme, saying that if we want to find true peace, we needed to follow the path of the Dhamma, the Way, the Truth. And to help us in this we should practice the teachings of the Buddha. In particular, living by the Five Precepts and the Four Cardinal Principles as we seek to live meaningfully and well in this human realm.

THE FIVE PRECEPTS

Abstention from killing any sentient beings

Abstention from taking what is not given

Abstention from sexual misconduct

Abstention from telling lies and slanders

Abstention from intoxication

THE FOUR CARDINAL PRINCIPLES

Instead of causing suffering to a fellow human, efforts should be made to relieve him of any mode of suffering and render him peaceful and comfortable. Do good things for the benefit of others in need. Try to observe the Four Cardinal Virtues of the mind:

Loving kindness to all

Compassion to all

Rejoicing at someone's success

Equanimity (even-mindedness) and

detachment (caring non-attachment)

THE CAUSES OF SUFFERING

Greed, hatred and delusion are the cause of all suffering. We need to refrain from greed or anger, and we should try to help the needy without expecting any sort of return. To overcome these negative emotions, we must practice tolerance and loving kindness.

HUMILITY

Never let one's view or belief go to the extremes; use wisdom to seek the truth and come to terms for peace.

Refrain from thinking that only my view or my concept is the correct one. Matters should be discussed amicably to reach a point of common interest. We should all be aware that each one of us is going to grow old, diseased, and eventually to die. This understanding of our own mortality should reduce one's conceit and arrogance.

He ended by repeating that if all humanity practised the above then everyone would live in peace and be secure all over the world. '*I wish that all humanity could see the truth and find peace.*'

The following day we were awake by five after only a few hours' rest, not sleep. Work started at six.

Later that afternoon I was sitting with Phongyi and Ma Lwin Lwin Htoo, one of the bright girls who had been part of our initial computer class. I hadn't seen her much since the first computer classes at the monastery, as she had often left to help her parents when her 19-year-old brother unexpectedly died during an asthma attack and there was no medical facility nearby. At times like this I knew we would somehow have to work out a way to provide more medical help to the community.

All of a sudden, the factory manager came running towards us shouting and waving.

'*Please come quickly, the engineer is ready to connect the water supply!*'

We all ran to the factory. I could see that the work team had performed a miracle – all the filters had been installed, the air conditioning was up and running, and the bacterial tests had been done. Even the new water samples had already been taken, sealed and made ready to send for detailed testing in the laboratory in Yangon. As we arrived, the engineer turned on the switch and the purified water came gushing out of the filters and poured all over the floor – we had forgotten to put the bottles in place! But it hardly mattered. We were all too excited. We cheered and hugged each other. We felt we had moved mountains. It was truly a momentous occasion, one of the most joyous moments of my life. I gazed on the faces of the children. Their smiles said it all.

That evening we returned to the hotel at Nampan, and as the sun slowly set beneath the horizon, I thought my journey, too, was coming to an end. The orange glow cast a magical carpet of fading light on the still waters of the lake. I stood looking out from the comfort of my hotel towards the monastery and reflected on the lives of the children living there. This incredible journey had brought me to a country where so much seemed to be changing and yet that seemed as far away from my world as ever.

The children are all our futures and so by helping them we help ourselves. I came here as a tourist and am leaving as someone enriched by the experience. I know that I will return. Just as the sun will rise again in the morning, so too will the dreams and aspirations of those children. We have done something to change their lives. But I know there is more, much more, we must do. This is not the end of the journey. So often when horizons seem to close, we find that it is the time when they are opening.

'You cannot travel the path until you have become the path itself'

Buddha

CHAPTER 14

PRAYING

'Have compassion for all things,

rich and poor alike;

each has their suffering.

Some suffer too much,

others too little.'

Buddha

In my conversations with Phongyi I had strived to discover the secret of his calmness and serenity. How was he able to manage the lives of hundreds of children – to feed, clothe and educate them – with so little financial support? Why had I been so ridiculously stressed at times and struggled with the responsibility of juggling the demands of a comfortable if very busy middle-class life?

Although the sums may seem small to us they are enormous in a country where families in rural areas exist for a whole year on less than the price of an iPhone. For example, it costs £20 (US $30) to provide enough rice to feed 1000 children for one day and £200 (US $300) to pay the running costs of the monastery for a day; less than the price of a night at some hotels in London or New York. Far less.

There are basically three monks who manage the monastery with the help of a handful of teachers; plus administration staff, volunteers, novice monks and students. To discover more I asked if I could to shadow a number of monks, teachers and children through a day in the life of the monastery – in order to try and learn something about what made Phongyi so special.

His day, and therefore mine, began at 4.30 am in the open courtyard of the monastery.

It was a cold late December morning – probably close to freezing in the open air. As I entered I saw Phongyi sitting facing the image of Buddha deep in meditation. There was a mat next to him as a silent invitation for me to join him. I sat in meditation, I didn't know for how long, perhaps thirty minutes. Then he turned towards me and for the next fifteen minutes or so we held hands and with our eyes closed meditated together with love and compassion for all humanity. It was a truly profound experience.

METTA PRAYER OF LOVING KINDNESS

May all beings be peaceful.

May all beings be happy.

May all beings be safe.

May all beings awaken to the light of their true nature.

May all beings be free.

I felt the Ko Yin (novices) quietly entering the area and taking their places around us, again in silence. Then the other children arrived. Phongyi turned to the children and said a few prayers, and the children then began chanting. After the deep meditation my mind was very receptive and the harmonies resonated like currents of electricity through my being. It was hugely uplifting. The prayers and chanting finished and we all meditated together for another fifteen minutes or so. Afterwards the children seemed energised, smiling and happy. It felt like a good start to the day.

From the prayer area the children made their way to the open field behind the monastery where they formed up in lines for morning exercises. These looked to me to be a mixture of Saluting the Sun sequences and military drill. I thought this was probably a useful synthesis of the teachers and monks day-to-day experiences from their overlapping worlds of war and peace. There was a lot of laughter and while they were obviously working the children were also having great fun.

Breakfast started just after 6 am following which the children made their way to the classroom block where lessons continued throughout the day until 4 pm, with a short break for lunch. After the karma yoga of household duties the children met up again in the monastery area at 5.30 pm for a short religious education class. Phongyi reminded them of moral values and emphasised the monastery mantra:

- Be honest
- Help others
- Try your best in every endeavour

By 8 pm the children had finished dinner and disappeared to their quarters for self-study. They were probably asleep by 9 or 10 pm, when the monastery fell silent.

The system of school education is exactly the same throughout Burma – primary school from 5-10 years old; middle school from 11-14 years old; high school from 15-17 years old. The main subjects, all taught in Burmese, are maths, history, geography, science, Burmese literature and English as a language. The monastery inculcates a volunteering spirit and encourages a culture of charitable activity and loving kindness. Consequently most students aspire to become teachers, nurses and doctors.

Those who pass with merit at around 17 years old are placed straight into government schools as teachers following a short period of three months or so training. Others who wish to progress to college or university to study a profession, especially medicine, are given help by the monastery. The fees are now subsidised by the government but the accommodation and living costs can amount to US $100 per month per student, which the monastery has to find. Phaya Taung provides the spiritual support, education and training, and social welfare services for the whole locality. Without this monastery, most children – including the most talented – would have very few prospects for their future.

I asked about meditation and learned that as part of the daily routine all the children at the monastery are taught and practise simple anapana-sati meditation from an early age. The Buddha laid special stress on this in-and-out breathing meditation method, for it is the gateway to the path to enlightenment. The idea was to instruct them on shamatha, or calm abiding, and give them the tools to bring tranquility to the mind.

I asked Phongyi about his own meditation. Something I had been keen to discover but only recently tried. What type of meditation did he practice and could he teach me?

The first thing he told me was that meditation is not a ritual. It is a source of teaching and wisdom.

He had chosen to follow a type of meditation called Vipassana, one of India's most ancient techniques. Vipassana means insight into the true nature of reality, and the reaching towards the unceasing clarity of mind that has no reality of its own, so the mind in meditation is free. It was rediscovered more than 2,500 years ago. It involves observing the way you breathe to concentrate the mind and sharpen your perceptions. As Phongyi described it to me then, it seems to have little to do with faith, intellect or philosophy and everything to do with coming to terms with facing life's problems in a wise, calm, and balanced way. It is the process of self-purification and observation.

I wanted to find out more of this, and was relieved to discover that it is open to anyone and everyone, and that you do not need to convert to Buddhism in order to practise it. But Phongyi was unable to teach me and suggested I look for those with the experience of passing on the technique in a professional environment. I resolved to do just that when I returned to the UK.

A day or two later, when I had finished everything I could do to help at the monastery, I set out back to London. As always after a visit to Phaya Taung and the children, my head was full of plans and the challenges we faced. I had started this journey in 2009 with a family visit to my wife's birthplace at Taunggyi and seen a new venture born at a remote monastery and orphanage on the shores of Inle Lake. What began as a quest to source computers for the children had ended with building a water bottling plant. Not only would all the children now have access to safe clean drinking water but the monastery would be able to sell the surplus, which would help meet the cost of their education and food. But with more and more children seeking both sanctuary and education, there were going to be growing demands on the stretched resources.

Almost from the outset, the water purification and bottling plant proved to be a real success. Along the way we had to change the design of the labels to remove the image of the young monks in order to avoid offending strict Buddhists. Discarding empty water bottles portraying images of monks was upsetting some people, who felt it was disrespectful. At one stage there was talk of taking us before the religious council. Phongyi was shocked, too, because he had endorsed the original design. In the end it was easier and more prudent to redesign the label, which we did.

Purified water is now being piped from the mountain spring three miles away, and is freely available from a row of taps installed outside the plant for the children and local village people to use for drinking water. Ko Yin bottled water is already being sold within a five mile radius of the monastery. We are working towards extending the distribution network and reaching further afield. The good news is that the water has excellent nutrients, with a ph level of 7.8 (The acceptable range is 7-8.5) and an amazing fresh and natural taste. There are now around 1,200 children including 1,000 boarders at the monastery. Its future, and that of the children, will depend on the continued faith and belief of those that are responsible for running it.

My mind turned to reflecting on the lives of the children at Phaya Taung. I thought about Mayawk (the monkey) and how his life had changed because of the love he had been shown. He is now one of the happiest children at the monastery. He attends school and is doing well. He still loves his sweets, but only occasionally. It seems only yesterday he was a shy and hopelessly lost soul with a grim past and a bleak future.

And then there's May Than Nu, the student who had told us her own harrowing story. From being a quiet and introverted girl, she has blossomed into a confident young lady, extremely dexterous with computers, so much so that she is now the computer teacher and manages the Computer Club. Who would ever have imagined it? The daily computer classes are flourishing not just as a teaching aid, but also for all the administration work of the monastery. I have been so impressed by the skill of the children and the teachers and in the standard of work being done. Recently, the monks have moved the computer classes to a new purpose-built schoolroom that will also house a library. This is progress indeed.

I kept thinking of Ma Lwin, who had lost her 19-year-old brother because of the asthma attack he had succumbed to without any medical care nearby, and of the needs of so many children there suffering from infectious skin diseases and other ailments.

And let's not forget our genius pupil San Aung. In just three days he had managed to master the principles of computing, and begun to understand computer programmes to an astonishing degree. This is a world where he has a rare and natural talent, and as a result he is no longer a novice, but is working hard to improve his skills as a student at the monastery school.

Sadly, he became very ill after contracting a skin disease resembling ringworm. It is a condition that normally can be treated quite easily, but he simply hadn't been able to get to a doctor. Like water, we take access to medical care for granted, but when you are living in parts of Burma, it's a luxury.

I couldn't help but wonder if his condition was somehow the result of coming into contact with his contaminated surroundings. What we see may look innocuous enough. What we eat may taste good enough. What we drink may refresh us. But the truth is that for so many people very little that is to do with their health can be taken for granted. One of the greatest needs, other than access to safe drinking water, is ready access to health care.

And so began the next stage.

During the visit I had suggested that we explore the possibility of building a Health Clinic. This could provide medical care for the children as well as an emergency service for the local villages. Ting and I sketched out a rough plan for the building and, once we were happy with the draft concept, Ting went on to draw up the plans and work out all the building costs.

The original design for a basic clinic was adapted to incorporate an adjoining room and bathroom for visiting doctors or specialists and volunteers from abroad. Our philosophy was not only to cure patients, but also to provide health education for the children, and raise awareness of the best ways to prevent disease. Malaria, cholera, diarrhoea – the biggest killers – can all be prevented or at least reduced through having a better understanding of their causes. We were determined to start.

CHAPTER 15

PERSEVERING

'As rain falls equally on the just and the unjust,

do not burden your heart with judgements,

but rain your kindness equally on all.'

Buddha

During January 2015 I set to work raising funds for the Health Clinic. It turned out that we had good momentum going for us on the back of the success of the launch of Ko Yin water. Existing Inle Trust donors were happy to help once again, and in particular the Paul Foundation was very supportive. We were oversubscribed, and so with mutual agreement the Rangoonwala Foundation earmarked funds for a future sanitation project for the Phaya Taung community. We were thrilled – we could turn our dreams for the children into reality.

I returned to Burma in March 2015, this time with my daughter Sumaya who wanted to spend some time in the classes teaching art to the children. I was excited. I felt we were building on a strong foundation at the monastery, and we now had both the energy and the funds for the Health Clinic as well as ideas about how best to provide basic health education for the wider community. Ting and I agreed the final plans with Phongyi and so, the very next day, after a prayer ceremony, we began the construction work on the clinic building itself.

We had seven months to find a medical team to set it up and get it going. I knew we could achieve this – but my background training told me that the main issue was going to be how to pay to keep it staffed and running. After some thought I hit upon an idea. The room used for storing the medicines could be divided to give separate access from the outside, and we could set up a pharmacy. Conventional and herbal medicines could then be sold to the public. That was one idea, but an even better one came one day when I was enjoying a cup of green tea and a chat with Phongyi.

My tea tasted a little bitter and so Phongyi suggested adding some honey to it. He passed me one of our water bottles into which he had poured some local honey – and with the taste of it came the very next opportunity for Phaya Taung.

'If we could clearly see the miracle of a single flower

our whole life would change.'

Buddha

Phaya Taung Monastery honey! It was in plentiful supply, as were the herbs grown by the monks. We could harvest and sell green tea, garlic, turmeric, lemon & ginger honey, all making good use of the monastery's Ko Yin brand. We could market it as 'Ko Yin Wild Honey'. Not only would it be nutritious but the herbs would also help provide relief from common ailments like coughs, colds and stomach upsets. It could be sold via the pharmacy as a health product, as well as to nearby hotels, restaurants and shops alongside the Ko Yin mineral water.

One of my favourite quotes comes from Rumi, the great Sufi philosopher.

'What you are seeking is also seeking you'

Rumi

I now I began to experience this. On leaving the monastery with my daughter Sumaya I was wondering how on earth I could persuade a doctor from England, who had experience in tropical medicine, to come over and set up the clinic and get it going. I had heard from Phongyi about a doctor from France, who had made a fleeting visit to the monastery a year or so earlier and said she may well come back, but Phongyi had no means of contacting her. Phongyi suggested I go to the hotel in Nyaung Shwe, run by a Frenchman called Pierre, who just may have a way of connecting with a fellow national.

So on the way to the airport at HeHo to catch our flight to Yangon, we stopped over in Nyaung Shwe, the small town right on the north of Inle Lake. After making some enquiries we were shown the way to Pierre's hotel. As it happens he was on a visit to France, so I left a copy of my book and my contact card with a note asking if he knew anyone who could put us in touch with the doctor. It seemed like a very long shot.

We continued on to HeHo airport, where I sat outside the airport terminal near the runway, taking in the last of the spring sunshine. After a while I noticed a woman – the only other person outside – walking towards me. I thought she was about to ask for a light for a cigarette, as this was also the unofficial smoking zone, but she wanted to know if I had any information on the status of the flight to Yangon, which had by now been delayed.

We started to chat and I told her about our work at the monastery. I had become unashamedly opportunistic by now to tell people about Phaya Taung, and always tried to sell a copy of my book. I asked her to give me her email so I could send her a link, and she could then read all about it. When she scrolled down her email it was @doctors.org.uk. I couldn't believe it. I laughed and said, 'You will regret that you gave me this!'

What I realise now is that in this short space of time, from leaving the monastery to arriving at the local airport, *what I was seeking had already sought me out.*

This was pure serendipity – as a result of our chance encounter, over the coming months both Dr Isabella Salmona from France and Dr Jane Dunbar from Scotland contacted me and volunteered their help and expertise, and were actually present at the setting up of the clinic. They both worked tirelessly over the days leading to the opening – not only making sure we had a fully operating clinic, but holding seminars with the children on disease prevention and first aid. Before the formal opening in November they had hosted three surgeries and treated some two hundred patients. Most importantly, Dr Isabella had located in a nearby village a fully qualified nurse, who was experienced in local diseases and therefore ideally suited to manage the clinic. As if to complete the circle, my editor and friend Andrew Thorman, when he had visited the monastery a few months earlier, had made a commitment that he would fund the wages of a nurse.

Phongyi was right.

'If you want to succeed, you need to use all your God-given faculties and also at the same time make your own luck.'

The universe had delivered far beyond expectations – not one doctor but two!

When I returned to London in March, I had already decided to enroll in a Vipassana retreat. I had been thinking a lot about what Phongyi had told me about his meditation practice, and I was determined to find someone to teach me.

I should explain that for some years now I had been friends with a spiritual master. In fact, we had been friends for some fifteen years before we started talking about religion and belief, or anything spiritual. It was through him that I had first been introduced to meditation in any form whatsoever, and he taught me the principles of Zikr. Around 2009, just before MuMu and I set out on our very first trip to Taunggyi, my friend had said to me that I must be ready for anything. We talked at length about matters of faith and the living of life, and I do remember feeling a sense of liberation. On parting, he had said to me:

'You cannot know the truth by reading, studying, lecturing, thinking – close those doors. Only then in stillness the doorway of the heart will begin to open up'.

Over the years of our friendship my spiritual master showed me that the spiritual path is a direct path towards self-knowledge and an understanding of the true nature of reality. Following it is the way to live a full life, and cultivate a wise heart. It is a path free from rituals. The miracle one experiences is the profound change and transformation to one's whole being as you discover the purity and luminance of spiritual love itself.

I had continued to live as I always had, imperfectly balancing work and family. But the miracle of landing in a rainstorm at Phaya Taung, and the way it changed my outlook, enabled me to begin to practice what I had been taught but never experienced. You might think it was an accident, but I believe it was meant to be. It was my karma. I was ready. In the early summer, I set out for The Art of Living Vipassana Meditation retreat in rural Herefordshire, close to the border between England and Wales, for ten days of study and meditation in silence according to the teachings of S N Goenka (a Burmese-Indian teacher of Vipassanā meditation). The rules were straightforward: no killing, no stealing, no sex, no lies and no drinking. Just meditation. There was no communication of any kind with other students. Men and women were taught and housed in separate parts of the building. We were to dress simply. No books, cameras, recorders or anything that might distract from the teaching. We were woken at 4 am and meditated for two hours before breakfast. Meditation followed until we went to bed at 9.30pm with breaks for lunch and tea. My room was big enough for a single bed with a small window.

To begin with I wasn't sure I could last the course. But as time went by I found myself adapting to what must appear to anyone outside a very rigorous regime. My body and mind slowly but surely came to accept the routine. I left feeling many different sensations but very glad I had embraced the technique. From that time on I began to build regular practice into my daily life.

The course certainly sharpened my perceptions. I know I have become much more aware of my fellow beings and their feelings. I think I am more compassionate as a result. I found it really helped me to still my mind, and understand much more about the significance of living in the eternally unfolding present moment. So much stress is caused by imagining the future and clinging to the past, and forgetting that the present moment is all we have. But it has also made me more sensitive. You feel more pain, especially for others, because your senses are so much sharper. The big thing is realising that we are all mortal, and so we need to practice our mindfulness and live as fully as we can every single day.

After the retreat, I went to Italy for a holiday, and I was joined there by Andrew Thorman. He was there to help edit the new version of this book, and assist in filming my interview with Andrea Bocelli for the Discovering Humanity TV series. During the course of his stay he asked me what next at the monastery. Of course my thoughts had never left Phaya Taung, and since my retreat I had been gently wondering if I could help in any way with either education resources or facilities to increase the amount of meditation taught at the monastery. I was keen to do more to share my new-found experience in meditation. I said to Andrew it would be amazing if we could set up a Vipassana meditation centre at the monastery.

But it turned out that Phongyi was already way ahead of me, as I would find out on my next visit.

'I would like to find a way to improve the moral and mental health of our people,' he told me.

In his subtle way he was involving me in yet another phase of the monastery's growth. Once again, we were in lock-step on the path. By now I was convinced that although we didn't even speak the same language, Phongyi and I were cosmically connected to each other.

We returned to Phaya Taung in the autumn. As always, Phongyi had delivered beyond expectation. We saw in front of us a beautiful red-bricked building, complete with tiled flooring and treatment beds handmade by the local carpenter. There were also special quarters – in this case a room with a view and an attached bathroom – for visiting doctors to use while running the Clinic. And, believe it or not, right outside was a Red Cross sign with the word Clinic inscribed on it. Everything had been completed within our budget. It was an emotional and rewarding time for everyone involved. The children's Health Clinic opened formally on 24 November 2015 with much pomp and ceremony. All the village elders were invited, and all the teachers and children also participated. Dressed in colourful ethnic costumes everyone danced and sang together to the local music. There were food stalls and Ko Yin mineral water was sold by the bucketful. It was a joy-filled festival and a true celebration.

On the very same day The Inle Trust commissioned the building of 24 toilets, 10 showers, and improvements to the girls bathing areas. It's such a basic requirement for a community, and so easy to construct, but a lack of awareness and reliance on the natural environment had always inhibited progress.

Phongyi gave a most inspirational speech and asked me to speak. I wanted to emphasise that although I stood here today and enjoyed celebrating this very special moment with them – none of what we had achieved would have been possible without the support of my family and the help of so many people from many countries who had read about the children, and donated both money and services to this cause. I wanted to thank them as they, the children, thanked me. It was a very emotional occasion and there was a realisation that if we managed to get the workings of the Health Clinic right it would indeed be a turning point in the health and welfare of the children and the villagers.

Phongyi wanted to share this with all the villagers nearby, and make it known that they, too, could come for treatment at the monastery on their very doorstep, rather than have to make an expensive and often arduous journey to a hospital many miles away.

The sequence of events leading to this momentous occasion at Phaya Taung are inspiring – and even, I would say, magical. Why? Because whatever was sought just happened when it was called out for. It was good karma, in that each and every positive action led towards a positive result.

We now have a fully operating clinic at Phaya Taung where a

team of doctors from Khaing Myittar Hospital in Taunggyi visit regularly and treat the children and the villagers, and they are able to extend their treatment and care to communities well beyond the monastery and the village. Both of our founding doctors – our angels of mercy – Isabella Salmona and Jane Dunbar continue to make regular visits to the Health Clinic, and in conjunction with The Inle Trust are now involved in setting up a bursury fund to provide a scholarship for monastery students to train as doctors and nurses. In addition, Dr Isabella Salmona, who is also an ayurvedic medicine practitioner, has established a physic garden of herbs and vegetables at Phaya Taung, to help improve the diet and health of the children.

Later that evening Phongyi, Major and I sat to discuss the events of the day and what Phongyi said to me then was most uplifting.

'The practical needs of the 1200 children are now complete, Feroze. They have clean water to drink, there is money from the sale of Ko Yin mineral water to buy food. They have good education, a fine computer training facility, and now a medical clinic and sanitation facilities.'

But his words were also tinged with sadness. I could sense that he was telling me the time for building was passing. It was now time for the spirit.

I reflected on how much had been achieved in such a short period of time, and although I have been enthusiastically congratulated and have received several awards for the work involved, I know in my heart of hearts that I am a mere instrument - a figurehead - in the evolving process of change at Phaya Taung. In helping to facilitate what was needed to provide for the needs and the happiness of the children I was just one part of the karma – the cause and effect. One thing had led on to another, and people had appeared at the right moments to help, and events happened at the right time. For me it has never been down to chance or coincidence. This work is part of a divine plan, I am sure, undertaken with beauty and perfection.

I had come to understand that there is no beginning and no end if you follow the Dhamma. All that was happening was the realisation that every single one of my experiences at the monastery was made up of both giving and receiving, finding and letting go, dreaming and being. It was a part of me now. I was learning to let go my attachments and, thanks to Phaya Taung, grow spiritually and find genuine enjoyment. Bees feed on the nectar of flowers; they don't cling to the blossoms.

After a long pause, Phongyi continued. He said that he had built a small pagoda for meditation on the hillside a short distance away from the monastery. I instantly knew where we were going with this. He invited me to join him for meditation at 4 am the next morning at our normal place. This time we enjoyed Vipassana meditation together, and afterwards the children joined us for a session. When we had finished, Phongyi asked me to follow him to another new and special meditation room. Although it was a modest wooden structure, it was perched at the highest point on the monastery land overlooking the lake. We sat together and meditated, finishing just as the sun came up from the mountains. The view across the lake was breathtakingly beautiful. I was floating weightless, bodyless.

We did not talk but we communicated. We both knew that this was a perfect starting point from which to build a proper meditation retreat centre at Phaya Taung, where visitors and local people could come to learn and practice Vipassana meditation.

Phongyi's view of the practice of Vipassana meditation is very similar to that of Goenka, in that there are no prerequisites for anyone who wishes to learn and follow meditation. Such practice can help all people improve as human beings and lead to a more meaningful and happy life. On the way back from the monastery, Major made inquiries with local monks to try and identify and if possible visit a few monasteries where Vipassana meditation was practiced. It was not easy because such monasteries are quite rare these days. The nearest one was some 50 miles away from our monastery, in Hti Han Swe village in the Shan Hills. I wanted to find a monk who could teach at our centre in Phaya Taung when it was ready.

It took us a whole day of travel by boat and car to get there. When we arrived we were met by a very kindly monk called U Wasana Theika. The head monk was not present as he was away visiting another monastery. U Wasana taught meditation to the locals but said that most people don't want to spend a period of ten days (the minimum time needed to learn Vipassana) away from their daily lives, but he held quite a few one-day meditation training sessions. He reminded us that before one began the training and practice of Vipassana meditation it was essential that a human being observed the five moral precepts of Buddhism: abstention from killing, stealing, sexual misconduct, lies and slander, and intoxication.

In fact my observation, which was confirmed by U Wasana, was that the Burmese people have moved away from the essence of Buddhism – with ever decreasing amounts of time set aside for meditation. My later research showed that even many of the monks themselves do not practice Vipassana. Whilst the monastery system continues to flourish, to an increasing extent they provide much of the spiritual context for social festivals rather than providing meditation teaching.

I had separately begun some research on this topic back home in London in collaboration with the eminent psychiatrist Professor Dr Ahmed, visiting professor of psychiatry at the University of Karachi. He is a great believer in how meditation and prayer have a significant positive effect on brain pathways, and consequently their use in either the avoidance or treatment of many mental illnesses.

Major, his son Livingstone, the monk and I talked for a while at the Hti Han Swe monastery, and then we meditated together for fifteen minutes. By then it was getting late, so we left to make our way back to Inle Lake with a feeling of sadness that the treasures of Vipassana meditation were being lost by the very people who were masters at this practice not so very long ago. We had a new challenge ahead.

At present, the idea is to build a boarding house next to the Phaya Taung pagoda, so that visitors from far and wide can come to the monastery on meditation retreats in the months between November and April, when the climate is wonderful. During the other months of the year people from the local community can attend meditation courses.

'Meditation brings wisdom; lack of meditation leaves ignorance.
Know well what leads you forward and what holds you back,
and choose the path that leads to wisdom.'
Buddha

CHAPTER 16

REFLECTING

'Yesterday I was clever, so I wanted to change the world.

Today I am wise, so I am changing myself.'

Rumi

A s I pen the last lines of this book, the prophecy that Ahwin made when I first came to Taunggyi only a few years ago echoes in my ears. 'If you go to the lake your life will change forever.'

And so it has. My time from here on will be spent working for the well-being of the children at the monastery. They have captured my heart and my soul. I hope and pray that my efforts help change their lives for the better too.

My family and friends have on the whole been very supportive. I am a much calmer person. My children, I hope, prefer me as I am today. Although they think I can be a bit overpowering in terms of expressing my affection. I am probably a bit too tactile at times and perhaps that's seen as making up for the past.

Meditation has given me the ability to feel and understand more of what people are going through. Wisdom and knowledge comes from many different places but it is the wisdom inside you that really counts.

I have been incredibly lucky. I haven't had to move the ladder

I was climbing along to another wall, and start to climb up again from the bottom, as Joseph Campbell notably wrote. Arriving at Phaya Taung monastery in a rainstorm, looking for shelter while on a family trip with MuMu, was the best thing that could possibly have happened to me. I started to think differently and I began to learn what is truly important. Our time is limited, and I discovered that I needn't waste mine in living what was increasingly becoming someone else's life. Phaya Taung taught me I could continue growing, but in a better way, and gently move towards this most creative stage of being.

Everything changes, nothing remains the same – but that isn't how we consider things in the West. I found that by putting my energies into helping the monastery and the children, I was transformed in myself. I could have spent years searching – or even, heaven forbid, failing to move beyond my zone of comfort – yet by putting my energies into a new direction and accepting the changes involved, this new time of my life has become a destination. It was a hidden journey to begin with, but the shift in thinking and culture and teaching has enabled me to enter a different world. My key to transformation has been acceptance – to love, accept and serve the world.

Some people probably thought I was having some sort of crisis three-quarters of the way through my life. They may have thought that this was just a phase I was going through and that I would get over it. The determined pace of my progress towards the changes I have chosen to make, and the help I have tried to give, has alienated some people. I know that.

'You must accept the truth from whatever source it comes.'

Maimonides

If I had just retired from my business life, I know I would be lost. Instead I have found a new beginning. The work at Phaya Taung has given me a purpose and a passion. It is true that I had the experience and capacity to help realise the dreams we had to make the monastery self-sufficient for the children, but in doing this I discovered the most important thing of all, which is that if you keep your mind open, you can learn too. The moment you stop learning you grow old. Not just physically, but mentally.

My wife MuMu often felt sidelined by what was happening at the monastery. At times she felt this was my journey and not hers. I think – I know – this put a strain on our relationship. She told me on more than one occasion that I was becoming obsessed to the exclusion of all else, including her feelings. I had put my heart and soul into helping those children and I couldn't stop. But at the same time I knew I had to be more considerate at home and recognise that I could not have done it without MuMu. Whilst I have been totally passionate about what I have been doing, I hope and believe that the whole experience has been profoundly good for all the family – even though sometimes it caused strain at home. For example Nadir, my son, has occasionally been skeptical, not so much about the meditation, more about my spiritual feelings. He's training to become a psychologist so he's allowed to feel that way!

Coming to terms with so many emotional challenges – the plight of the children, the uncertainties in dealing with Burmese bureaucracy and the need to embrace the support and love of my family – at times were overwhelming.

Without knowing where it would lead, at Phaya Taung I opened a door onto my mind, and went through it. Now I have a different kind of life, with new priorities. In return for all we achieved at Phaya Taung, I have been given a gift so remarkable, something I could never have dreamed of: peace, tranquility, an immense deep happiness, the lessons of loving kindness and the burgeoning of spiritual love. Anyone with goodwill and sincerity can experience this change for themselves.

I was anxious to ask Phongyi his thoughts on how to live life more meaningfully, balancing our search for happiness in this world with the essence of home and work. He smiled.

'Happiness comes to your heart through your ways. Change the way you behave and improve as a human being.'

That's all well and good I said, but how exactly do we change our ways?

'Have discipline. Have principles in your life. Keep to them. They are your pillars,' he said.

And so, during the six years that have passed since MuMu and I first visited Inle Lake, the balance has shifted and the rhythm of my life is very different. But it took me quite a while to understand.

My work in London was getting in the way of my dreams for Phaya Taung, and I knew I had to find a way out without letting down my clients. I had to find another perspective to match my new feelings and priorities. Phongyi had wisely told me not to be impatient and not to become frustrated or angry.

'Helping others through your own efforts can achieve a true level of inner satisfaction and real spiritual happiness,' he said.

He is so right, and I am again reminded of my father and MuMu's father who were both so generous in life and so happy because of it.

'Doing good for others provides them relief from their pain – this is inherent in human nature.'

Phongyi's words left me with a lot to think about. Since returning to London, I have never stopped thinking about the people I encountered in Burma, especially the children. They are the future and they deserve to drink safe water.

Would I do it all again? Without question. We are all searching for our true path. We may not set out to do so but I firmly believe that it is in our DNA. What triggers success or failure, misery or happiness, frustration or fulfilment is entirely in our gift. I never expected to spend five years of my life working to help children in a far-flung corner of the world. I did not set out in life with a sense of philanthropic giving. I did not dream that one day I would embark on a journey which would lead me to the deep peace of meditation. Ahwin's prophecy to me has turned out to have been more of a blessing. I feel as if I have been given another chance at doing something with my life.

Many people have helped me along the way, especially my family. Without their love and support I would never have been able to achieve what has been done at Phaya Taung. My family is everything to me and I would go to the ends of the world to keep them safe. The profound – and wonderfully surprising – benefit of Vipassana meditation has helped me to ease the tensions that had caused me such stress in my life, and to evaluate everyday situations in a more balanced and calm manner. I try to find a time every day to meditate, develop insight, and work on improving my practice.

People sometimes say to me that all we have achieved so far could have been done without nearly so much involvement from me, but I think that misses the point. People who know me know I will not give up and, inasmuch as I do this for myself, I hope it is not in a selfish way. The health and happiness of the children is reward enough.

'It's not how much we give, but how much love we put into giving.'

Mother Theresa

What I learned was that by working together with the monks at Phaya Taung and getting to know the children, we were able to do much more than we could ever have imagined from a desk in London. The lives of the children have become a part of us now, and hopefully we have helped them build a lasting and sustainable future on solid foundations.

I have been given so much by the children, and I have benefited beyond anything money could buy. The words of my father come flooding back. *'If you live by charitable deeds you are giving to God and he will always repay you.'* He was so right.

There are many reasons to be optimistic about Burma's future. Tourism and foreign investment are providing the kind of resources that will change the face of the country forever. But the greatest hope can be seen in the faces of the children who expect so little and who give so much.

High in the hills of Tuscany in Italy is a Catholic monastery called La Verna where I go to find peace. I discovered it some years ago and every time I go there I take time to count my blessings and concentrate my thoughts on the children we are helping. It is a wonderful place where I can recharge and renew. I know I will never be able to manage to match Phongyi's commitment but then I don't know anyone who could.

Working with Phongyi and the children at Phaya Taung has been a bridge into another life for me. From the shore by the monastery I threw a small pebble into Inle Lake and watched the ripples forever widening. One journey comes to an end, but the journeys of the spirit are just beginning.

POSTSCRIPT 1 –
THE BEAT GOES ON ...

Discovering that humanity has a caring heart is a wonderful antidote to the suffering caused by conflict in the world today. I am now on a mission to meet and discover more of these kind, compassionate and thoughtful people who are helping to make a difference. I want to learn from them and share their experiences and understand their motivation. Recently I decided to develop a TV interview concept and we now have a six part TV series whereby such remarkable people share their wisdom and experience so that others may learn and follow.

I recall the words of Anne Frank, the German-born Jewish girl who died of typhus in Belsen Concentration Camp aged just 16. In her famous diary she wrote: ' No one ever became poor by giving.'

But what I have discovered while researching and filming these interviews is that there are very many people who have been inspired to make a difference. Some of them are famous – like the blind Italian opera singer Andrea Bocelli whose foundation is helping fellow sufferers in Africa, and the 'Angel of Mercy' Abdul Sattar Edhi, a penniless peddler who founded the Edhi Foundation, the largest non-profit social welfare organisation in world. I've also been lucky enough to meet Kishwar Naheed, the feminist Urdu poet who fought to receive an education when it was denied to women in Pakistan, as well as the Danish faith healer Damaris Lau and another great opera singer Joseph Calleja, who lives in Malta and whose foundation helps abandoned and deprived children. I have also met Clive Stafford-Smith, the brilliant founder of the charity Reprieve which saves death row prisoners from execution. These people are all helping to change people's lives.

POSTSCRIPT 2 – POLITICAL UPDATE, DECEMBER 2017

For more than 40 years between 1962 and 2011, Burma was ruled by a military junta which suppressed almost all dissent andwielded absolute power in the face of international condemnation and sanctions. The generals who ran the country stood accused of human rights abuses, including the forcible relocation of civilians and the widespread use of forced labour. The first general election in 20 years was held in 2010. This was hailed as an important step in the transition from military rule toa civilian democracy, though opposition groups alleged widespread fraud and condemned the election as a sham. Despite this inauspicious start to Burma's new post-junta phase, a series of reforms in the months since the new government took office led to hopes that decades of international isolation could be coming to an end. This was confirmed when US Secretary of State Hillary Clinton made a landmark visit in December 2011 – the first by a senior US official in 50 years – during which she met both President Thein Sein and Aung San Suu Kyi. President Obama followed suit in November 2012, and hosted President Thein Sein in Washington in May 2013, signalling the country's return to the world stage. The EU followed the US lead, lifting all non-military sanctions in April 2012 and offering more than $100m in development aid later that year. Ceasefire deals signed in late 2011 and early 2012 with rebels of the Karen and Shan ethnic groups suggested a new determination to end the long-running conflicts, as did a draft ceasefire agreement signed between the government and all 16 rebel groups in March.

Aung San Suu Kyi finally swept to victory in November 2015 on a tide of hope and excitement in Burma's first truly democratic election for 25 years. Her success followed more than 50 years of oppressive military rule and, it was hoped, would herald a new era of freedom and reform. Burma has been at war with itself ever since the British handed over power to her father General Aung San at the end of the Second World War. A coup in 1988 saw the military tighten its grip on the country and less than a year later Aung San Suu Kyi was placed under house arrest. Elections in 1990 saw her National League for Democracy (NLD) party returned to power but the junta refused to concede. Despite growing international condemnation of the Military's role in Burma, Aung San Suu Kyi was effectively to remain a prisoner in her own country until 2010.

Her triumph at the ballot box in March 2016 is now being considered by many as hollow – with much of the international community disillusioned by the lack of promised reform. It would seem that Aung San Suu Kyi has limited power as, although her NLD party won a landslide victory taking 86% of the seats in parliament, they were powerless to elect their leader to be head of the government. Constitutional law precludes anyone with a foreign spouse or children from becoming President, and Aung San Suu Kyi was married to the British academic Michael Aris with whom she has two children. The constitution, too, was altered to ensure the military would always remain in control of the country's political future. Any legislative voting in parliament requires a majority of 75% plus one, and so, given the military has 25% of the seats enshrined in law, it effectively holds a lifetime veto.

To attempt to circumvent this, on 30 March, 2016, Parliament, sitting in Burma's purpose built capital Napyidaw, chose to elect a puppet President, Mr Htin Kyaw. He is a loyal supporter of Aung San Suu Kyi who, in the role of State Counsellor, is widely perceived to be in control of the agenda. But although the 'Lady', as she is called by her adoring supporters, won the political fight – she is struggling to win the peace and there is increasing frustration and dismay at the lack of reform.

Hundreds of thousands of people – mainly the Muslim minority who live in the western state of Rakhine bordering India and Bangladesh – were denied voting rights. Fighting flared up between Buddhists and Muslims, with many fleeing across the border to Thailand to escape what they claimed was persecution and worse. The NLD has not embraced its Muslim population – far from it. The party considers many to be illegal migrants and thousands are reported to be held in transit camps.

At the time of the 2016 election, the international community remained relatively passive in terms of openly criticising the new government about the treatment of its ethnic minorities. Everyone was watching with a mixture of fear and hope. But through the following year the situation in Rakhine State has become truly shocking and developed into a humanitarian crisis on a colossal scale. The Burmese military launched an offensive on the Rohingya population, citing the need to retaliate to attacks by Rohingya terrorist groups, which has now displaced well over 600,000 people, killing civilians indiscriminately and burning villages, and pushing refugees towards the border with Bangladesh. There are now over 1 million Rohingya refugees in camps across the border, and the UN has condemned the action as text-book ethnic cleansing and it believes that Burma wants to expel its entire Rohingya population.

And there are tensions elsewhere too, in this fragmented, largely rural and still undiscovered country - in Kokang, for example, between ethnic minority rebels and the army - while floods and landslides have continued to claim lives. Meanwhile the frustration at the lack of progress on promised reforms has seen student protests in Yangon with dozens arrested.

International reaction has focussed on pressuring Aung San Suu Kyi to condemn the atrocities in Rakhine State and at the same time re-imposing sanctions on the economy. The West struggles to respond. Burma is balanced between the hopes of only two years ago for this mesmerisingly beautiful but poor country and its graceful people, and the realisation that the moral authority of Aung San Suu Kyi can only be diminished while behind her the military remains entrenched in power. The challenges are immense for Burma which the historian Thant Myint U described as 'a country broken by 20 years of sanctions, 30 years of self-isolation and 50 years of authoritarianism'. And we have a broken dream.

Burma's economy is crucial to the development of the country. The army and the NLD will have to work in partnership if they are to capitalise on Burma's rich abundance of natural resources, and that is going to mean compromises – on human rights as well as foreign investment. The army may resist concessions over what it sees as hard-fought battles to control the country's warring factions.

Meanwhile the Chinese are queuing up at the border to invest in the country's infrastructure. Already there are myriad signs of Chinese influence in Yangon, with new hotels and office buildings as well as housing schemes springing up everywhere.

Within the rest of the country – where subsistence living is the norm – the story is very different. There's a tangible lack of progress. But perhaps this has also been why so many people want to visit the country – to enjoy and experience one of the last places in South East Asia to embrace the world of high-rise hotels and glitzy neon-lit shopping malls. Burma's innocence lies hidden in its jungle-clad mountain ranges, its largely peaceful nature, and strikingly beautiful and yet relatively unspoilt landscape and coastline. Tourism has tripled in the last five years to more than a million visitors a year. The discontent and flare ups in ethnic tension have so far been mostly confined to areas which attract few foreigners. The majority of visitors are unaware of the turbulent political undercurrent which threatens to halt the progress of democracy. There remain parts of Burma that are still out of bounds to visitors because of the continued fighting, drug smuggling and poor communications. Air travel is the most reliable way of accessing many towns and cities. The road system is in desperate need of modernisation, while the railway system seemingly belongs still to the colonial era.

As one chapter closes, another opens. The new parliament is not representative, and the authoritarian power of the military is undiminished. But there is much freer speech and certainly peace has come to some of the regions. There are freedoms in business to help broaden prosperity and work is being done in the education system and to some of the infrastructure. Time is needed for healing and trust, and the danger remains that the army will not allow the nascent freedoms to flourish. Key ministries like home, border affairs and defence remain under military control. As Aung San Suu Kyi said: 'It is not power that corrupts but fear. Fear of losing power corrupts those who wield it and fear of the scourge of power corrupts those who are subject to it'.

APPENDIX 1: BACKGROUND INFORMATION

1. Lake Inle is a freshwater lake located in the Shan Hills in Myanmar (Burma). It is the second largest lake in Myanmar with an estimated surface area of 44.9 square miles (116km2), and one of the highest at an altitude of 2,900 feet (880m). During the dry season, the average water depth is 7 feet (2.1m), with the deepest point being 12 feet (3.7m), but during the rainy season this can increase by 5 feet (1.5m). The watershed area for the lake lies to a large extent to the north and west of the lake. The channel between Nampan going south to Samkar (2nd lake) and further 3rd Lake at Pekhon was just a creek known as the 'Belu Creek.' Belu means Ogre (because the rock from which the creek starts looks like the mouth of an Ogre). In 1967 the Moepye Damn was built near Pekhon by the military government which flooded and devastated a lot of farm land and villages including Thar Kaung village and parts of Samkar and caused the creek to balloon into Lakes. There is a hot spring on its north-western shore.

2. Most of the ethnic minorities in Myanmar live along the country's mountainous frontiers. Karen and Shan groups comprise about 10% each, while Akha, Chin, Chinese, Danu, Indian, Kachin, Karenni, Kayan, Kokang, Lahu, Mon, Naga, Palaung, Pa'O, Rakhine, Rohingya, Tavoyan, and Wa peoples each constitute 5% or less of the population.
   Source: Burma Campaign UK

3. With an approximate length of 2400km, the Salween River is one of the longest rivers in the region. It flows through several countries, originating on the Tibetan plateau in the Himalayas, then passes through Yunnan Province in China, down through Shan and Kayah States in Eastern Myanmar), along the border with Thailand through the States of Kayan and Mon before emptying into the Gulf of Martaban in the Andaman Sea. Source: Salween Watch.

4. The Burmese Communist Party (BCP) White Flag faction was located in Pegu Yoma while the Red Flag faction was based in Rakhine State (formerly Arakan State). Both were Communist underground groups later assimilated by the government.

5. The Wa National Army (WNA) was headed by former Wa Chieftain Mahasang, and fought for the leadership of the Communist Party of Burma (CPB).

6. The Karenni National Progress Party (KNPP), the largest Karenni (Kayah) group in the jungle, was an anti-Communist group formed following the 1875 treaty between Burma and Britain. The military arm of the KNPP (The Karenni Liberation Army) was involved in an armed struggle with The Burmese Communist Party (BCP), the Kayah New Land Revolutionary Council and The Karenni People's United Liberation Front. The Kayin (Karen) National Union (KNU) was founded in April 1947, and is the oldest ethnic insurgent group. The military arm of the KNU was The Karen National Liberation Army (KNLA). Its leader was the Mon National Defence Organisation (MNDO) many of whose members, like the KNU, lived in Thailand sometimes joined General Bo Mya. *Source: United States Bureau of Citizenship and Immigration Services- August 2002.*

7. Taunggyi is the capital of Shan State, and is the fifth largest city in Myanmar with an estimated population of 205,000 (as of 2010).

It is 4,712 feet (1,436m) above sea level.

APPENDIX 2: THE ETHNIC, RACIAL AND RELIGIOUS PROFILE OF BURMA

Burma (Myanmar) is an ethnically diverse nation with 135 distinct ethnic groups officially recognised by the Government. These are grouped into eight major national ethnic races:

1. Kachin
2. Kayah
3. Kayin
4. Chin
5. Mon
6. Bamar
7. Rakhine
8. Shan (includes Pa'O and Intha)

These races or tribes are grouped primarily according to the areas where they live rather than by their linguistic or ethnic affiliation, for example the Shan Major National Ethnic Race includes 33 ethnic groups speaking languages from at least four widely differing language families.

APPENDIX 3: THE PA'O PEOPLE

The Pa'O form an ethnic group comprising over half a million people. They populate the States of Shan, Kayin, and Kayah. The Full Moon of Tabaung is celebrated as the Pa-O National Day. The Pa'O are largely Theravada Buddhists. It is believed they settled in the Thaton region of present-day Myanmar about 1000 B.C. They were enslaved, and forced to wear indigo-dyed clothing, to signify their status. Today there are many regional variations of clothing worn. The Pa'O predominantly engage in agriculture, cultivating leaves of the thanapet tree (Cordia Dichotoma) and mustard leaves. They have largely assimilated into Bamar society, adopting many of their traditions.

The Pa'O Legend

It is said the Pa'O migrated from Central Asia but there is no authenticated record of their origins. The legend of Weikja and Naga has been adopted as their ancestry.

Weikja was a wise and powerful warrior who could fly through the air and Naga, who could change into a beautiful human form, turned into a dragon when she fell asleep. When Naga came to visit the earth as a young woman she met Weikja. They fell in love and went to live together in a cave. Naga became pregnant and after falling asleep Weikja returned to find a dragon in his bed. Heartbroken he flew away from earth forever. When the time came Naga laid two eggs. She gave them to a pious monk to look after. The eggs cracked open and the monk began to peel them to reveal a human body in the form of a boy in one egg and a girl in the other. And so the name Pa (crack) and O (peel) came into being. The boy became the first King of Thaton – the Land of Gold. Tradition requires that Pa'O women wear two ornaments in their headgear representing the head and eye of the Naga dragon. Their clothing is layered with leggings and longyis (sarongs) under a long shirt and short coat representing the scales of a dragon. The Pa'O were one of the earliest converts to Theravada Buddhism in South East Asia and remain devout Buddhists.

Pa'O Recent History

After the British left Burma in 1948 many of the ethnic minorities in the country began to form groups to promote their independence and to rid the country of the influence of the feudal Sawbwas' gambling and opium dens. The PNO had already been established in 1946-47 as a resistance movement against the

Shan Sawbwas. It later joined forces with the Karen insurgents. In the early 1950s they became the largest insurgent force in Burma operating against government forces in the mountains round Taunggyi and Inle Lake.

A peace settlement was brokered in 1958 in return for the promise of local democratisation. Soon after, all the Shan Sawbwas gave up their powers in return for government compensation. This included a locally elected Shan State Government based in Taunggyi with the authority to raise local taxes and with responsibility for health, education and law.

On 2 March 1962 Prime Minister U Nu was ousted by a military coup putting an end to the development of federalism and democracy. The Pa'O remobilised. The new leadership renamed the PNLO (PNO) as the SSNLO (Shan State National Liberation Organisation) and recruited troops from other ethnic groups including Shan and Karenni. In the 1960s and early 1970s they enjoyed limited success against government held towns. However Communism was gaining ground at the time, including within the SSNLO, causing an ideological rift between the Communist and Nationalist factions within the party.

In 1974 the Nationalists split from the SSNLO (Red Pa'O) to form the SSNLF (White Pa'O or PNO). Fighting started between these two groups in the Southern Shan State. Villagers were caught between the two warring factions and the government forces. The much-weakened Pa'O became largely ineffective. In 1978 the PNO established a small military presence on the Thai border near Mae Hong Son funded by bribes from cattle smugglers. In 1983 the SUA (Shan United Army) successfully attacked the PNO camp crippling the Pa'O military and economic activity in that area. In 1987 the government cancelled certain bank notes more than halving the value of currency in circulation and sparking further unrest.

Many students joined the PNO but could not endure the conditions. Although the Red and White factions within the PNO attempted to settle their differences on several occasions they proved impossible to reconcile with past atrocities. In 1991 the PNO signed a ceasefire with the SLORC (military government) and in return were able to retain their weapons and local militia. Inter alia, the PNO was also granted mining concessions and agreements to operate tourist hotels at Lake Inle south of Taunggyi.

The PNO is now also a political party and has onemember in The Upper House and three members in The Lower House of the National Assemblies and six members in the Shan State Regional Assembly. It is currently working with the government to establish Pa'O self- administration in the townships of Pin Laung and Hshiseng. The PNO continues to press for improved economic and welfare conditions in the region.

Source: *The Pa'O Rebels & Refugees – Russ Christensen & Sann Kyaw.*

APPENDIX 4: THE INTHA PEOPLE

The Intha (also known as 'sons of the lake') are members of a Tibeto- Burman ethnic group living around Lake Inle. They speak an archaic dialect of Burmese and are believed to have come from the Dawei area. They number some 70,000 and live in four cities bordering the lake, in numerous small villages along the lake's shores, and on the lake itself. The entire lake area is in Nyaung Shwe Township. The population consists predominantly of Intha with a mix of other Shan, Taungyo, Pa'O (Taungthu), Danu, Kayah, Danaw and Bamar ethnicities. Most are devout Buddhists, and live in simple wooden stilt houses woven from bamboo. They are largely self-sufficient farmers.

Most transportation on the lake is traditionally by canoe though more and more are being fitted with outboard motors. Local fishermen are known for practicing a distinctive rowing style involving standing at the stern on one leg and wrapping the other around the oar. This unique system of sculling was developed so they could see over the vegetation that covers large areas of the lake surface. It is only practised by the men. Women row in the customary style, sitting cross-legged at the stern.

CHILDREN OF THE REVOLUTION

PICTURE CAPTIONS

KO YIN MINERAL WATER

The water factory at Phaya Taung Monastery started operating on the 20th of August 2014. It now provides purified mountain spring water of the highest quality currently to the 1,200 children at the monastery and the surplus water is bottled and sold to the public to provide funds to feed the children. One bottle sold feeds one child one meal. Without the help and support of all of our sponsors this would not have been possible. However, there is still much to do, and your continued help is very much needed if we are to achieve all our ambitious plans for these very deserving people.

MAP OF INLE LAKE

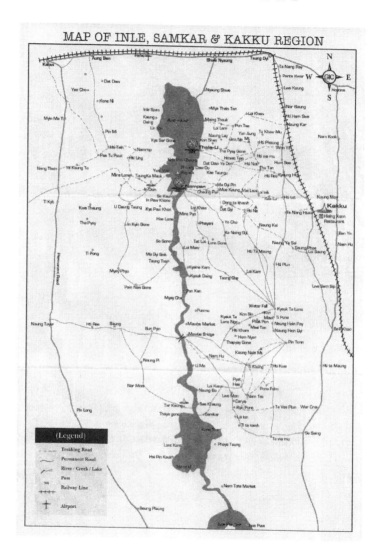

THE OBJECTIVES OF THE INLE TRUST CHARITY

The relief of poverty and the preservation and protection of good health of people living in Phaya Taung and elsewhere in Myanmar and developing countries, in particular by providing or assisting in the provision of water and sanitation projects, hygiene, education, training and all the necessary support designed to enable individuals to live a healthy life. The Inle Trust is a Charity registered in England, number 1154767. Email: trustees@inletrust.org.uk

MAP OF BURMA